Difficult Passages in the Epistles

Robert H. Stein

BAKER BOOK HOUSE
Grand Rapids, Michigan 49516

Printed in the United States of America

Library of Congress Cataloging-in-Publication Data

Stein, Robert H., 1935–
Difficult passages in the Epistles.

Includes index.
1. Bible. N.T. Epistles—Criticism,
interpretation, etc. I. Title.
BS2635.2.S74 1988 227′.06 88–8005
ISBN 0–8010–8293–5

 Other versions cited include the King James Version (KJV), the New American Standard Bible (NASB), the New English Bible (NEB), and the New International Version (NIV).

To **Bill** and **Syl**,
Duane and **Helen**,
Ann, **Jan** and **Jim**

Contents

Preface

A number of years ago I began a series of articles in *The Standard,* the denominational journal of the Baptist General Conference. With the encouragement of the editor, Donald E. Anderson, I discussed various difficult passages found in the canonical Gospels. These articles were then published by Baker Book House in 1984 under the title *Difficult Passages in the Gospels*. Upon completion of that series Anderson suggested that we might do a series on difficult passages in the Epistles of the New Testament. Having finished that series, I was encouraged to place it also in book form as a companion volume. The kind reviews of the former work have also encouraged me to make these materials more readily available for readers.

I want to thank once again my wife, Joan, for her reading these materials both as series articles and now in this present form. I have always valued her helpful criticisms and suggestions. I also want to thank my colleague, Tom Schreiner, and my teaching assistant, Daniel Nold, for their careful reading of the manuscript.

Introduction

The difficulties which a reader encounters in the Epistles tend to be quite different from those encountered in the Gospels. One reason for this is the difference in their literary genre. In the Gospels we encounter the genre of historical narrative. Along with the task of understanding what the author is seeking to teach by the historical materials, there enters into consideration the historicity of these materials. How do the accounts recorded in these works correspond to what actually happened? Was Quirinius really governor of Syria, and was there really a census under Quirinius when Jesus was born? Was Jesus really tried before the Sanhedrin, Herod, and Pilate? By their very nature the study of the Gospels brings historical issues to the surface.

The Gospels also present the reader with certain difficulties in that there are multiple accounts of various events. At times we have four separate accounts of an incident. At times we have close parallels in the three Synoptic Gospels. Yet these accounts are never exactly the same word for word. It is clear that the Evangelists thought of themselves as inspired interpreters of the life and teachings of

Jesus and not simply as stenographic secretaries, and thus the differences do raise questions for the reader. Along with these problems we also encounter difficult sayings, actions, and predictions that come from the lips of Jesus.

In the Epistles (or Letters) of the New Testament we encounter a different set of issues. We are not involved so much here in asking, "What really happened?" as in seeking to understand the meaning of the author in his historical context. We are, of course, interested to learn all that we can about the thought-world of the first century and especially of the early church, but there are far fewer allusions to historical circumstances and events in a book like Romans than in a book like Luke. And for the most part the questions that parallel accounts raise in the Gospels are absent from the Epistles. The issues we meet in the Epistles are more linguistic in nature, and in this work we shall seek to illustrate how one can come to understand the meaning which an author gave to his words. In *Difficult Passages in the Gospels* it was pointed out that many of the difficulties that we encounter in reading are resolved once we understand what the author meant by his words. This is equally true in the case of difficulties encountered in the Epistles.

In this book we shall begin with the most basic building block used by the writers. We shall look at how we can understand the meaning an author gave to *words*. This will be our area of concern in chapter 1. In chapter 2 we shall deal with how to understand the statements in which these words are found. Here we shall point out the importance of the *grammatical syntax* which an author gives to his words within the statement. In chapter 3 we shall emphasize the importance of the *authorial context*. By the words, sentences, and paragraphs with which an author surrounds his statements, he gives important clues and hints as to what those statements mean. We shall look at how the authorial context helps us to understand various difficult statements found in the Epistles. In chapter 4 we shall look at the *larger context* of the entire biblical canon and see how our knowledge of this context enables us to understand and resolve various difficulties. In the final chapter we shall look at an example in which we can apply each of the principles learned in the first four chapters as well as consider how to deal with an example which seems to defy a successful resolution.

1

Understanding Words

The basic building blocks of all statements are words. Since all statements are constructed of these basic building blocks, an incorrect understanding of the meaning of an important word in a sentence will inevitably lead to an incorrect understanding of the sentence. As a result, one of the primary tasks of interpretation is to understand what the words of a statement mean, or as one author has stated, we must "come to terms." Only then can we proceed to the meaning of the statement itself. Since, however, one cannot spend a great deal of time investigating every individual word in each sentence, the interpreter must focus attention upon the key terms. These are fairly apparent by the frequency with which they appear in the sentence and its immediate context as well as by their importance in the argument.

People have used a number of methods in order to understand the meaning of words. One such method is the study of the etymology of the word. What is the root meaning of the word? The reader may even have heard sermons in which reference is made to the root meaning of the English word which is used to translate the Greek or

Hebrew term: "Webster's Dictionary tells us that this word comes from a root which means . . ."! Such a procedure is obviously faulty. The writers of Scripture were not thinking about the root meaning of English words that would be used to translate their texts millennia later. Yet, in a more academic fashion, scholars have also at times built on the root meaning of a Greek or Hebrew term in their text. In the vast majority of instances this is likewise an erroneous procedure. An example will demonstrate this. When speakers use words such as "nice" or "let," are they thinking of their root meanings? Or are they thinking of how these words are being used at the present time? Surely it is the latter. They are not thinking that the word *nice* comes from the Latin *nescius,* which means "ignorant," nor that in the eighteenth century "nice" meant "precise." And when they use "let," are they thinking of its Middle English root *lette,* which means "hinder" or "obstruct"? Note, for instance, Romans 1:13 in the King James Version: "I purposed to come unto you, (but was let hitherto)." Here "let" is used in its old sense of being hindered, but today we do not use this word in this manner except in playing tennis, where a "let" hinders the game from proceeding. The complete detachment of the present meaning of words from their etymology is most apparent in the attempt to understand the meaning of idioms. Idiomatic phrases have little connection with the root meanings of their words. This is why trying to understand the meaning of idioms in a foreign language is so difficult.

In general the etymology of a word is of little or no importance in understanding the meaning of that word in a statement. Writers usually have little interest in the root meaning of a word or the history of how the word has been understood in the past. They are interested only in how it is understood in the present. Using more technical terminology, we can say that writers pay attention not to the diachronic or past meaning of a term, but to its synchronic meaning at the time when they write. The etymology of a word is useful in two instances, however. One such instance occurs when an author intentionally plays on the etymological meaning of the word. Paul does this in Philemon when he plays on the name *Onesimus*, whose root meaning is "useful," and refers to the fact that once Onesimus was "useless" but now he is "useful" (v. 11). There are many times when the biblical authors play on the root meaning, that is, the etymology, of a name (e.g., Gen. 2:23; 3:20; 4:1; 17:5; Matt. 1:21, 23). The second instance in which the etymology of a word may be useful occurs when a word appears only once or twice in literature, and we do not know what its meaning is. In such cases when the synchronic or contemporary meaning of the term is unknown, the only possibility left for the scholar is the hope that when the author used this term, it still bore a meaning closely resembling the meaning of its root. Today this is not very likely, for the meanings of words change so quickly. Think of how such terms as "a square guy" (a compliment if my father said it), "gay," and "pot" have changed or taken on new meanings in the past few decades. On the other hand, ancient languages and society tended to be far more stable and traditional, so that biblical terminology did not experience such rapid and radical changes. Nevertheless, we should always remember that the use of etymology for understanding the meaning of a word, unless the author clearly indicates a play on the etymology of the word, is a last-chance attempt at trying to discover the meaning of the word in the author's time. It is in a sense a last resort. Certainly one would not want to build a theological argument on the supposition that a word bore the exact meaning of its ancient root.

There are several other pitfalls that can ensnare readers in their pursuit after the meaning of the words in a text. One pitfall is to assume that a word that looks and sounds alike in two different languages has the same meaning in both languages. This is less a problem for the biblical languages than for modern languages. (A friend of mine immigrated as a young child from Germany to the United States. He was frightened by the experience, especially when upon arrival he and his parents met a large, black immigration official, for the boy had never seen a black man before. The immigration official was a kindly gentleman and tried to befriend the lad. Offering him a candy bar, he urged, "Take it. It's a gift. Gift." Now my friend's fright turned to sheer terror, for in German "Gift" means poison!) A more serious problem lies in assuming that the range of meanings of an English word corresponds exactly to the range of meanings of the biblical word it translates. For instance, the word *pneuma* is translated by "spirit" in English and "Geist" in German, but the English word has potential meanings not possible in either Greek or German. Alcoholic "spirits" is possible only in English. (For an example of this kind of problem see pp. 21–26. An even more serious problem encountered in seeking the meaning of biblical words is created by the false assumption that a word possesses the same meaning everywhere it is found. Essentially this assumes that biblical words are technical terms whose meaning is constant for all biblical authors. (For an illustration see pp. 31–36.)

Individual words possess a range of possible meanings, and the same word can be used to mean quite different things. Five minutes' reading in a dictionary will demonstrate this. The word *love*, for instance, does not mean the same thing in every statement. In one sentence it can mean "affection"; in another it can mean "sexual intercourse"; and in still another "a score in tennis." The context alone determines which particular meaning (out of the whole range of possible meanings) the word has in a given statement. When using a word, an author generally chooses one specific meaning out of the possible range of meanings of that word. It is only through the context in which the word is found that we can understand the specific meaning of the word. Using more technical terminology, we can say that a word in the "norms of language" has a finite range of meanings. A dictionary provides us with this range of meanings or the *langue* of a word. In a statement, however, a word has a particular or singular meaning. The "norms of the utterance" limit these possibilities to a singular meaning or the *parole*. Thus whereas the *langue* involves all the possibilities which language permits (all the dictionary possibilities), the *parole* limits the meaning of the word to the single, particular meaning of the author (the one specific dictionary meaning the author intended, such as "a score in tennis").

The process by which the meaning of an individual word is determined by the context, and the meaning of the context is at the same time determined by the meaning of the individual word, is called the hermeneutical circle. Although it seems extremely difficult, in practice the process is quite simple. Within the mind the reader or listener is able to clarify the precise meaning of a word by understanding what the context reveals about the specific meaning of the word. At the same time the preliminary understanding of what the word can and may mean is helping clarify what the context means. As I write on my word processor, I see time and time again the light switching back and forth from one disc to another. In the interpretative process the mind does the same, switching back and forth from the word to the context, and from the context to the word, until the context reveals the specific meaning of the word, and the word clarifies the meaning of the context.

There are three basic tools available for understanding the meaning of a word in a statement. The first is a dictionary or lexicon, which reveals to us the possible range of meanings or the "norms of language." Unless an author reveals to the reader otherwise, the desire to be understood causes the author to use words within this possible range of meanings. If a word is used in a way in which it has never been used before and the reader has no indication of this use, communication is impossible. This is revealed quite nicely in the conversation between Alice and Humpty Dumpty in Lewis Carroll's *Through the Looking Glass*:

> "There's glory for you!"
> "I don't know what you mean by 'glory,'" Alice said.
> Humpty Dumpty smiled contemptuously. "Of course you don't—till I tell you. I meant 'there's a nice knockdown argument for you.'"
> "But 'glory' doesn't mean 'a nice knockdown argument,'" Alice objected.
> "When *I* use a word," Humpty Dumpty said, in a rather scornful tone, "it means just what I choose it to mean—neither more nor less."
> "The question is," said Alice, "whether you can *make* words mean so many different things."
> "The question is," said Humpty Dumpty, "which is the master—that's all."

Can Humpty Dumpty make a word mean whatever he wants it to mean? In his writings he can. *But* if he wants to communicate something to his readers, he is bound to abide by the norms of language and assign to words meanings within the acceptable range or boundaries. Although he may choose to give to certain words meanings outside those boundaries, he must reveal this to his readers, if he wishes to communicate. And since most writers seek to communicate their thoughts to their readers (why else would they write?), we can assume that the words they use have meanings lying within the norms of language. A dictionary or lexicon reveals to us the *langue* or possible meanings of each word.

The second basic tool is a concordance, which is most helpful in understanding what a particular word means in a specific instance. It helps by showing where an author uses this same word elsewhere. This in turn helps us to see if the author tends to use this term in a specific way. By this procedure we can narrow the scope of possible meanings to the specific range of meanings which an author gives to this word. It may even reveal instances in which the author uses this word in parallels whose meaning is quite clear. The third basic tool for understanding the particular meaning of a word is a grammar. Through this tool we better learn how a word functions in a particular statement. (Grammar will be the focus of chapter 2.)

Is New Testament "Wine" the Same as Today's Wine?

A good example of how misunderstanding develops by assuming that the meaning of a term in English corresponds exactly to the Greek or Hebrew word it translates is the word translated "wine" in the Bible. Does what we mean by the term *wine* correspond exactly to what the ancient writers meant by this word? Is the wine referred to in the Bible the same as that bottled today by Christian Brothers or Château Lafitte-Rothschild or Mogen David? The answer to this question is, "Not exactly." It is obvious that the term *wine* in the Bible does not mean unfermented grape juice, for the command "Do not get drunk with wine" (Eph. 5:18) and the numerous warnings against wine in Scripture (e.g., Lev. 10:9; Prov. 20:1; 21:17; 23:29–35) make no sense at all if the word refers to a nonalcoholic beverage. On the other hand, it is also clear that the term does not correspond exactly to what we mean by wine today.

In ancient Greek culture, wine was usually stored in large pointed jugs called *amphoras*. When wine was to be used, it was poured from the amphoras into large bowls called *kraters*, where it was mixed with water. This became clear to me when I had the privilege of visiting the great archaeological museum in Athens, where I saw dozens of these large kraters. At the time it was not clear what their use signified about the drinking of wine in biblical times. From these kraters, cups or *kylikes* were then filled. What is important to note is that before wine was drunk, it was mixed with water. The kylikes were filled not from the amphoras but from the kraters.

The ratio of water to wine varied. Homer (*Odyssey* 9.208–9) mentions a ratio of twenty parts water to one part wine. Pliny (*Natural History* 14.6.54) mentions a ratio of eight parts water to one part wine. In one ancient work, Athenaeus's *Learned Banquet*, written around A.D. 200, we find in book 10 a collection of statements from earlier writers about drinking practices. An exchange from a play by Aristophanes reads: "'Here, drink this also, mingled three and two.'/'Zeus! But it's sweet and bears the three parts well!'" The poet Euenos, who lived in the fifth century B.C., is also quoted: "The best measure of wine is neither much nor very little;/For 'tis the cause of either grief or madness./It pleases the wine to be the fourth, mixed with three nymphs." Here the ratio of water to wine is three to one. Other writers mentioned include Hesiod (three to one), Alexis (four to one), Diocles (two to one), Ion (three to one), Nicochares (five to two), and Anacreon (two to one). Sometimes the ratio goes down to one to one (and even lower), but it should be noted that such a mixture is referred to as "strong wine." Drinking wine unmixed, on the other hand, was looked upon as a Scythian or barbarian custom. Athenaeus quotes Mnesitheus of Athens:

> The gods have revealed wine to mortals, to be the greatest blessing for those who use it aright, but for those who use it without measure, the reverse. For it gives food to them that take it and strength in mind and body. In medicine it is most beneficial; it can be mixed with liquid and drugs, and it brings aid to the wounded. In daily intercourse, to those who mix and drink it moderately, it gives good cheer; but if you overstep the bounds, it brings violence. Mix it half and half, and you get madness; unmixed, bodily collapse.

It is evident that wine was seen in ancient times as a medicine (and as a solvent for medicines) and of course as a beverage. Yet as a beverage it was always thought of as a mixed drink. Plutarch (*Symposiacs* 3.9), for instance, states, "We call a mixture 'wine,' although the larger of the component parts is water." The ratio of water might vary, but only barbarians drank wine unmixed, and a mixture of wine and water of equal parts was seen as "strong drink" and frowned upon. The term *wine* or *oinos* in the ancient Greek world, then, did not mean wine as we understand it today, but wine mixed with water. Usually a writer simply referred to the mixture of water and wine as "wine." To indicate that the beverage was not a mixture of water and wine one would say "unmixed [*akratesteron*] wine."

One might wonder whether the custom of mixing wine with water was limited to the ancient Greeks. The burden of proof should probably be upon anyone who argues that the pattern of drinking wine in Jewish society was substantially different from that of the examples already given. And we do have examples in both Jewish and Christian literature and perhaps in the Bible that wine was likewise understood as being a mixture of wine and water. In several instances in the Old Testament a distinction is made between "wine" and "strong drink." In Leviticus 10:8–9 we read, "And the LORD spoke to Aaron, saying, 'Drink no wine nor strong drink, you nor your sons with you, when you go into the tent of meeting.'" Concerning the Nazirite vow Numbers 6:3 states that the Nazirite "shall separate himself from wine and strong drink." This distinction is found also in Deuteronomy 14:26; 29:6; Judges 13:4, 7, 14; 1 Samuel 1:15; Proverbs 20:1; 31:4, 6; Isaiah 5:11, 22; 28:7; 29:9; 56:12; and Micah 2:11. The 1901 *Jewish Encyclopedia* (vol. 12, p. 533) states that in the rabbinic period at least, "'yayin' [wine] is to be distinguished from 'shekar' [strong drink]: the former is diluted with water ('mazug'); the latter is undiluted ('yayin ḥai')."

In the Talmud, which contains the oral traditions of Judaism from about 200 B.C. to A.D. 200 (the Mishnah) and later commentary on those traditions (the Gemara), there are several tractates in which the mixture of water and wine is discussed. One tractate (Shabbath 77a) states that wine which suffers from being mixed with three parts of water is not wine. The normal mixture is said to consist of two parts water to one part wine. In a most important reference (Pesahim 108b) the writer states that the four cups every Jew was to drink during the Passover ritual were to be mixed in a ratio of three parts water to one part wine. From this we can conclude with a fair degree of certainty that the fruit of the vine used at the institution of the Lord's Supper was a mixture of three parts water to one part wine. In another Jewish reference from around 60 B.C. we read, "It is harmful to drink wine alone, or again, to drink water alone, while wine mixed with water is sweet and delicious and enhances one's enjoyment" (2 Macc. 15:39).

In ancient times there were not many beverages that were safe to drink. The danger of drinking water alone raises another point. The ancients could make water safe to drink in several ways. One method was boiling, but this was tedious and costly. They also tried different methods of filtration. The drinking of wine (i.e., a mixture of water and wine) served therefore as a safety measure, since often the water available was not safe. (I remember all too well drinking some water in Salonica, Greece, that would have been much better had it been mixed with sufficient wine or some other purifying agent.)

When we come to the New Testament, we find that the content of the wine is never discussed. The burden of proof, however, is surely upon anyone who would say that the wine of the New Testament is substantially different from the wine mentioned by the Greeks, the rabbis during the Talmudic period, and the early church fathers. In the writings of the early church fathers it is clear that "wine" means wine mixed with water. Justin Martyr around A.D. 150 described the Lord's Supper in this way: "Bread is brought, and wine and water, and the president sends up prayers and thanksgiving" (*Apology* 1.67.5). Some sixty-five years later Hippolytus instructed the bishops that they should "eucharistize [bless] first the bread into the representation of the Flesh of Christ; and the cup mixed with wine for the antitype of the Blood which was shed for all who have believed in Him" (*Apostolic Tradition* 23.1). Cyprian around A.D. 250 stated in his refutation of certain heretical practices:

> Nothing must be done by us but what the Lord first did on our behalf, as that the cup which is offered in remembrance of Him should be offered mingled with wine. . . . Thus, therefore, in considering the cup of the Lord, water alone cannot be offered, even as wine alone cannot be offered. For if anyone offer wine only, the blood of Christ is disassociated from us: but if the water be alone, the people are disassociated from Christ. . . . Thus the cup of the Lord is not indeed water alone, nor wine alone, unless each be mingled with the other. [Epistle 62.2, 11, 13]

Here it is obvious that unmixed wine and plain water were both found unacceptable at the Lord's Supper. A mixture of wine and water was the norm. Earlier (the latter part of the second century) Clement of Alexandria had stated: "It is best for the wine to be mixed with as much water as possible. . . . For both are works of God, and the mixing of the two, both of water and wine, produces health, because life is composed of a necessary element and a useful element. To the necessary element, the water, which is in the greatest quantity, there is to be mixed in some of the useful element" (*Instructor* 2.2.23.3–24.1).

Within the New Testament itself, we have only one example in which it is obvious that the author's understanding of *oinos* ("wine") differs from ours. This is found in Revelation 14:10 where the writer speaks of "the wine of God's wrath, poured unmixed (*akratou*) into the cup of his anger." Here it is clear that the author is speaking of an unusual display of the wrath of God. There is nothing normal about this display of God's wrath. It will not be mitigated by his graciousness. Rather, the "unmixed" pure wine of God's wrath will be manifested. If the author thought that the word *wine* meant what we mean by wine today, that is, pure wine unmixed with water, the use of the term *unmixed* would not have been necessary. However, since "wine" was normally a mixture of water and wine, he had to add the term *unmixed* to describe the undiluted wrath of God. It is evident from this example that in seeking to understand the meaning of a word we must seek to understand what it meant in the context of the author. The meaning of the English word used in the translation may not correspond perfectly with the meaning of the original word.

Can an Unbeliever Understand the Gospel? (1 Cor. 2:14)

One passage that has frequently been misinterpreted because of the misunderstanding of key words is 1 Corinthians 2:14. Here Paul states,

> The unspiritual man does not receive the gifts of the Spirit of God, for they are folly to him, and he is not able to understand them because they are spiritually discerned.

Frequently this verse has been interpreted to mean that according to Paul the non-Christian cannot understand the gospel message. An example of such interpretation is found in a recent work in which the author states, "Although God desires to communicate to all men, not just anyone can understand Scripture. . . . *Faith* is the prerequisite for truly understanding God's Word."

In order to understand exactly what Paul meant by his words, we must note the context in which they are found. This context is made up of numerous elements, including the historical period and the cultural milieu, but the most important element for narrowing down the range of possible meanings of Paul's terms is the author's own writings and in particular the immediate context. In regard to 1 Corinthians 2:14 this means that we should seek to understand what the terms in this verse meant in first-century Greek and in the situation of the early church of that period, but above all we must try to understand how Paul in his letters and particularly in 1 Corinthians used these terms.

With regard to 1 Corinthians 2:14 it will be especially important to note how Paul uses the terms *receive, folly, understand,* and *discern* if we are to interpret this passage correctly. For many people the term *folly* refers to "something which is not understandable, incapable of comprehension, unintelligible." Yet does "folly" deal with the mind's inability to conceptualize certain doctrinal statements, or does it involve an evaluative judgment of some sort? A closer look at how Paul uses this term elsewhere in 1 Corinthians is enlightening.

> Where is the wise man? Where is the scribe? Where is the debater of this age? Has not God *made foolish* the wisdom of the world? [1:20, italics added]

> For the wisdom of this world is *folly* with God. [3:19, italics added]

In the first example the apostle uses the verb form of this term (*emōranen*) whereas in the second example he uses the noun (*mōria*), but it should be observed that in both instances we are not dealing with a lack of comprehension or understanding. Surely Paul is not claiming that God is not able to understand the wisdom of this world. The omniscient God is certainly able to understand anything that the finite human mind is able to grasp. No, God understands the wisdom of this world, but he has judged and evaluated it as being foolish. To interpret "made foolish" and "folly" as evaluative judgments on God's part makes far better sense than to interpret them as meaning that God cannot understand the wisdom of this world, for Paul certainly believed that God is all-knowing.

First Corinthians 2:14 should be understood in a similar way. From experience it is evident that unbelievers can understand the doctrinal teachings of the Bible. In fact some unbelievers can describe and explain Christian doctrines better than some believers can. They can even get better grades on biblical and theological examinations. But (and this is no small ''but'') the unbeliever in evaluating these doctrines thinks that they are ''folly.'' Such a person judges them as unrealistic, primitive, superstitious, mythical, unscientific. In other words the unbeliever, although capable of understanding what these doctrines teach, is incapable of appreciating their truthfulness and significance. The believer, on the other hand, is convinced of their veracity and ascribes to them great significance, for to him these doctrines are truths from God himself. They are for him divine wisdom.

Another term that needs to be understood more clearly in this verse is the Greek word which is translated ''receive.'' In the Pauline Letters we find several instances in which it is used in the same sense as we find it here.

> And you became imitators of us and of the Lord, for you *received* the word in much affliction, with joy inspired by the Holy Spirit. [1 Thess. 1:6, italics added]

> And we also thank God constantly for this, that when you received the word of God which you heard from us, you *accepted* it not as the word of men but as what it really is, the word of God, which is at work in you believers. [1 Thess. 2:13, italics added]

> Working together with him, then, we entreat you not to *accept* the grace of God in vain. [2 Cor. 6:1, italics added]

In these examples the Greek word translated ''receive'' in 1 Corinthians 2:14 is rendered ''received,'' ''accepted,'' and ''accept.'' It is evident that in these examples to ''receive'' does not mean to comprehend or understand, but rather to welcome or to receive eagerly. Thus what Paul is saying in 1 Corinthians 2:14 is that the unbeliever does not receive the gospel message in the sense of welcoming it. This does not mean that he cannot understand the gospel message, but rather that his attitude toward and reception of it is hostile.

In a similar way the term "understand" (*gnōnai* in the Greek, "know" in the KJV) can mean more than to "understand conceptually." The range of meanings of this word in different contexts can be seen in the following passages:

> For although they *knew* God they did not honor him as God or give thanks to him, but they became futile in their thinking and their senseless minds were darkened. [Rom. 1:21, italics added]

> For since, in the wisdom of God, the world did not *know* God through wisdom, it pleased God through the folly of what we preach to save those who believe. [1 Cor. 1:21, italics added]

In both these instances the apostle uses the term which is translated "understand" in 1 Corinthians 2:14. In the first example Paul states that there is a sense in which the world possesses a conceptual knowledge of God's existence and power as witnessed to by his creation. In this sense the unbeliever "knows" God. Yet in a deeper sense the unbeliever chooses not to "know" God because the world does not delight in the gospel message. The world's wisdom has no room for the truth of its sin, its depravity, its helplessness. The wisdom of God, the cross, is simply folly to the world, and thus it chooses not to "know" God.

And so, in the context of this letter, to "understand" in 1 Corinthians 2:14 does not mean to "conceptualize" or to "intellectually comprehend," but rather to "grasp the truthfulness of" and to "recognize as fact." In this verse "understand" is used in conjunction with "discerned," which means "evaluated" or "judged." (See how the Greek word translated "discerned" here is rendered in

1 Cor. 2:15; 4:3–4; 9:3; 10:25, 27; 14:24.) To "understand" therefore means to evaluate positively. It is in this sense that the unbeliever cannot "understand" the things of the Spirit. Only when one possesses the Spirit can one evaluate correctly the truthfulness of the gospel message.

As a result of a proper understanding of various words in 1 Corinthians 2:14, we have interpreted this verse as meaning that the unbeliever, being unable to evaluate correctly the gospel message, judges it to be foolish, rather than as meaning that the unbeliever cannot intellectually understand Christian doctrines. This interpretation also accords well with the context of 1 Corinthians 1:18–2:5. Here Paul contrasts the wisdom of God, which the world denigrates as folly (1:18), with the wisdom of the world, which despite its cleverness (1:19) and lofty words (2:1) God has exposed as truly foolish (1:20). The issue in the first chapters of 1 Corinthians does not involve the ability of believer and unbeliever to conceptualize the Christian teaching concerning the death of Christ, but rather the unbeliever's attitude to this divine truth and God's rejection of the human-centered wisdom of this world. Paul does not deprecate wisdom in the true sense, for true wisdom does not stem from this world but from God (2:6–7). Paul, like the psalmist, deprecates a so-called wisdom that lacks reverence and submission to God, for he realizes that "the fear of the LORD is the beginning of wisdom" (Ps. 111:10). Apart from such reverence and submission the gospel message becomes a stumbling block to Jewish expectations and folly to Gentile philosophical reasoning (1 Cor. 1:23).

Perhaps what Paul teaches in 1 Corinthians 2:14 can be summarized by way of the following example. Imagine that a great professor, the world's leading Pauline scholar, is delivering a lecture on the apostle's doctrine of justification by faith. It is the most brilliant lecture ever given on the subject. In fact, if the apostle Paul had been present, he would have responded, "Thank you, Professor, for help-

meant by his teaching on justification, the professor adds, "But you know, of course, that this is pure nonsense!" It is clear that the professor as an unbeliever does understand Paul's doctrine of justification by faith. He can brilliantly conceptualize and explain this biblical teaching, but he does not welcome it. On the contrary, he rejects it as folly. What he lacks is the believer's Spirit-given conviction of the truthfulness and reality of this teaching.

On the other hand, imagine that a believer who lacks academic training is also asked to explain what Paul means by the doctrine of justification by faith. This individual apologizes for not being a theologian and, as tears form in the eyes, states, "I guess it means that Jesus did it all for us." Now it is evident that there is a sense in which the latter individual "understands" (i.e., is able to conceptualize) this great biblical doctrine far less than does the great professor, but there is also a sense in which the believer "discerns" it (i.e., recognizes its truthfulness) far better. "The unspiritual man does not receive the gifts of the Spirit of God, for they are folly to him, and he is not able to understand them because they are spiritually discerned."

Does James Disagree with Paul on Justification? (James 2:14–26)

The one biblical passage that has probably caused more theological difficulty than any other is James 2:14–26, for it seems to conflict with and contradict the Pauline doctrine of justification by faith. We need only place the two teachings side by side to see the problem:

> For if Abraham was justified by works, he has something to boast about, but not before God. For what does the scripture say? "Abraham believed God, and it was reckoned to him as righteousness." [Rom. 4:2–3]

> Was not Abraham our father justified by works, when he offered his son Isaac upon the altar? [James 2:21]

And

> For we hold that a man is justified by faith apart from works of law. [Rom. 3:28; see also 4:5]

> You see that a man is justified by works and not by faith alone. [James 2:24]

It is not surprising that Martin Luther, in seeking to make clear the Pauline doctrine of justification by faith, thought that the Epistle of James was "a right strawy Epistle" which contained no gospel.

The proper application of the basic principle that words possess a certain elasticity and therefore a range of possible meanings, so that the same word may be used in varied ways in different contexts, helps to alleviate the problem. For example, the English word *faith* can mean any of the following: a religion (the Hindu "faith") or a branch thereof (the Protestant "faith"); a specific set of theological doctrines (a church's statement of "faith"); a living, vital trust in God (she has a real "faith"); a set of intellectual tenets one ascribes to with varying degrees of commitment (one's "faith" in a number of causes); something which one believes is true but to which one nevertheless remains uncommitted or opposed (the "faith" of demons); an assured hope and trust (Heb. 11:1). The word *faith* can mean any of the above and more. As in the case of Humpty Dumpty (p. 20), the elasticity of a word, however, has its limits, for if we seek to communicate with others, the meaning we give to a word must lie within the accepted norms of language held by the community with which we are seeking to communicate. If we use a word in a totally new way, so that it means something outside the common norms of meaning, we must reveal this clearly to our audience if we want communication to occur. The word *faith*, for example, may mean any of the possibilities listed above, but it cannot mean "hamburger."

It is a false and dangerous assumption to believe that a word must always mean the same thing. Words can have a variety of meanings according to the context in which we find them. This is most evident when we look up a word in a dictionary. Usually there are a number of possible meanings for any given word. On the other hand, when a word is used in a specific context, it loses its elasticity and takes on one specific meaning. (In some instances a word can mean more than one thing, as in the case of a pun, but this is the exception to the rule.) A good example of how a word loses its elasticity in a context is the use of a sentence in a dictionary definition to illustrate one of the possible meanings of a word. In the sentence the word is no longer elastic but takes on a singular meaning. In view of the multiplicity of possible meanings caution must be exercised when we use a Bible concordance. It is indeed a most valuable tool, but we must not conclude that a word means the very same thing in all of its appearances in the Bible. The specific meaning of a word depends upon the specific context in which it is found. This is true for the Bible as well as for any other literary work.

Keeping this principle in mind, we shall now consider whether the terms *faith* and *works* have identical meanings for Paul and James. Looking first at the use of ''faith,'' we see that Paul speaks of an obedient trust (Rom. 1:5), a faith like Abraham's (Rom. 4:9, 16), a faith from the heart (Rom. 10:9), a faith involving discipleship (2 Cor. 5:7), and a faith that is accompanied by the gift of the Holy Spirit (Gal. 3:2, 14). On the other hand, we find that in James ''faith'' means something quite different. He speaks of a faith unaccompanied by works (2:14), a faith that can see Christians in dire need of food and clothing and not provide them with these necessities of life (2:15–17), an intellectual assent to a fact (2:19a), and a faith that even demons possess (2:19b).

We should also note the differences between the use of the word *works* by Paul and by James. For Paul "works" are antithetical to faith (Rom. 4:2–5) and to the grace of God (Rom. 11:6), involve the keeping of the Jewish law and in particular the rite of circumcision (Gal. 5:2–4), are a legalistic attempt to achieve a right standing before God by one's keeping of the law (Rom. 3:20; 4:2), permit one to boast before God (Rom. 4:2), and seek to place God in one's debt (Rom. 4:4). For James, however, "works" are acts of compassion done in obedience to faith, such as clothing the naked and feeding the hungry (2:15–17), are intimately associated with Abraham's faith (2:22), involve obeying God's direct command (2:21), and include protecting God's messengers (2:25).

It is evident that although both Paul and James use the terms *faith* and *works* within the norms of meaning for their day, in the specific context in which they wrote they selected different meanings for these terms. When Paul talks about faith, he means the believer's wholehearted trust in and sole dependence on the grace of God in Christ for salvation. James, however, means an intellectual assent to doctrine which neglects works of Christian love and which even demons possess. Clearly they are not talking about the same thing. As for "works," in Paul the term refers to self-righteous acts done legalistically in order to merit or earn salvation, whereas in James it refers to loving acts of kindness done by a believer who already has exercised saving faith.

So then, although the words of Romans 4:2–3 appear to conflict with those of James 2:21, and Romans 3:28 with James 2:24, in actuality they do not, because they do not bear the same meanings. Paul is attacking the view that one may be justified on the basis of works done legalistically in order to merit favor with God. Can we by our works place God in our debt? Paul argues vigorously that we are saved on the basis of God's grace and through faith alone. On the other hand, James in his epistle is attacking a totally different view. He is arguing against the position that mere intellectual assent without an accompanying rebirth issuing into newness of life can bring salvation.

Think for a moment how we might counsel identical twins, one of whom thinks that he must earn his salvation and will get to heaven only when he becomes good enough, and the other of whom thinks that despite all of his immorality and sin he will still get to heaven because ten years ago he made a "decision" for Christ. Would not we tend to share the Pauline emphasis with the former and the emphasis of James with the latter? Actually Paul's statement, "For in Christ Jesus neither circumcision nor uncircumcision is of any avail, but *faith working through love*" (Gal. 5:6, italics added), is quite similar to what we find in James 2:14–26. By understanding the principle that words contain a range of possible meanings and that the specific meaning of a word is determined by the context in which it is used, we alleviate much of the alleged tension between James and Paul.

There are at least two other reasons why this passage in James should not be interpreted as contradicting the teachings of Paul. These might better be dealt with in chapter 2 since it deals with the importance of grammar and syntax in interpreting a text. For convenience' sake, however, since we are dealing with this passage, we shall discuss them here. One additional argument in favor of our understanding of this passage is found in the hypothetical nature of James 2:14, "What does it profit, my brethren, *if* a man says he has faith but has not works? Can his faith save him?" [italics added]. In the original Greek we find a conditional statement in the subjunctive rather than in the indicative mood. Such a statement in the subjunctive mood deals with possibility rather than actuality. This means that James is not assuming that one can in fact have faith without works. Rather he is dealing with a hypothetical situation. To word this in another way, James is not implying that in reality a person can have faith but not works, for he assumes that this is impossible. A true faith is always associated with works of love (see James 2:18, "Show me your faith apart from your works, and I by my works will show you my faith"). Hypothetically, but only hypothetically, will he entertain the possibility of faith without works.

Second, we should note that in verse 14 James raises a question not concerning faith in the true sense but concerning the faith just spoken about, that is, the faith that has no works. In the Greek text there is an article present in the question, "Can his [lit., the] faith [we have just spoken about] save him?" This means that James is not talking about genuine faith as he understands it, but about an inauthentic faith—a faith without works. James asks, "Can the faith just referred to, that is, a faith which is unaccompanied by works of love and compassion, can this kind of faith save him?" The answer is, of course, no! Such a faith cannot save anyone. We are indeed saved by faith alone, but as one scholar has put it, the faith that saves is never alone. It always results in acts of loving obedience. As Paul states, only a faith which works through love can save (Gal. 5:6).

While no attempt has been made to explain all the difficulties that James 2:14–26 raises, the above insights alleviate some of the difficulties associated with this passage. Once we recognize that although the same terms are used by both James and Paul, these terms mean quite different things in their respective contexts, then we are well on the way to resolving some of the problems. This receives additional support from the hypothetical nature of the argument in verse 14 and the fact that James makes clear that *the* faith he is referring to is a counterfeit faith unaccompanied by good works, which is a faith even demons possess.

It is clear from the passages discussed in this chapter that a proper understanding of a biblical statement depends on a correct understanding of the meaning of the basic building blocks of that statement. Only when we understand what the author means by the words he uses can we come to understand what he means by his combination of those words into sentences. In seeking to understand the meaning of a word, the first step must be to delimit the range of possible meanings that a word may have. What is the semantic range of possibilities, or to phrase this differently, what do the norms of language allow as meanings for this word? A dictionary or lexicon is most useful at this point, for it will delimit the semantic range. Next we must eliminate various possibilities until we ascertain the specific meaning of the word in the sentence. Here a concordance, which helps us see how the author uses this same word elsewhere, and a grammar, which helps us to understand the grammatical construction of the immediate context, are most useful. When we know the specific meaning of various key words, we can go on to investigate the meaning of the statement or proposition in which these words are found.

2

Understanding Grammar

After we have come to understand the meaning of the individual words which make up a statement, we can proceed to the interpretation of the statement itself. A statement consists of a number of words which the author has put into some sort of grammatical relationship in order to express his or her thought. To understand the author's statement, the reader must decipher the grammatical code tying these words together. Although the reader might know precisely what each word in a sentence means, there is the additional problem that different combinations of these words can mean different things. For instance, the words *Joan, Bob,* and *loves* permit all sorts of possible meanings. We can say (1) Joan loves Bob; (2) Bob loves Joan; (3) Bob, Joan loves; (4) Joan, Bob loves; (5) Loves Joan Bob; and (6) Loves Bob Joan. These possibilities can be further increased by the way in which the sentence is punctuated. If we end them with a question mark, a period, or an exclamation point, we have additional possibilities of meaning.

Different languages use different grammatical codes. In English, word order is of paramount importance. The question of whether "Joan" is the subject or the object of the verb depends on its position in the sentence. In other languages, word order is of minor importance, and the relationship of a noun to the verb is determined not by word order but by its specific ending. Other aspects such as tenses, moods, and cases may be indicated by prefixes or suffixes. Often key relationships between parts of sentences are indicated by conjunctions or particles such as "if," "because," "when," and "in order that." Without a correct understanding of the grammatical code used by the author, misinterpretation is all too likely to occur. On the other hand, interpretative difficulties can frequently be resolved by a correct analysis of the grammar which binds words together. Whereas in the understanding of words, a dictionary/lexicon and a concordance are the most helpful tools, here the primary tool is a grammar. For the student of the Greek New Testament this will include a basic grammar of New Testament Greek and an intermediate or advanced grammar which deals with Greek syntax. For the student of the English Bible, the primary tool will be an English grammar. In this chapter we shall look at several examples in which a knowledge of Greek grammar plays a most important role.

What Does It Mean to Work Out Your Own Salvation? (Phil. 2:12)

One of the most precious teachings of the Christian church is the doctrine of justification by faith. In contrast to the idea that salvation comes through one's own works or through a combination of faith and works, the Reformers proclaimed that justification is a gift of God and that it is appropriated "by faith *alone*."

That this is a biblical teaching is evident. Above all, it was made clear by the apostle Paul, who struggled against the teaching of certain Judaizers. These Judaizers claimed that justification results from a combination of faith and works, and insisted that the Gentile converts to Christianity had to perform certain works, such as submitting to circumcision and keeping various Old Testament food regulations, if they were to be saved/justified (Acts 15:1–5). Paul argued vehemently against this teaching by pointing out that since the Gentile believers had by faith alone received the Holy Spirit, who is the firstfruits and seal of salvation, they did not need to do anything more. God had accepted them, and this was confirmed by his having given them his Spirit (Gal. 3:1–5; see also Acts 11:2–18; 15:7–11). Paul also pointed out that Abraham, the father of the faithful, was justified by faith alone (Gal. 3:6–9). Paul made several other statements to the same effect:

> For by grace you have been saved through faith; and this is not your own doing, it is the gift of God—not because of works, lest any man should boast. [Eph. 2:8–9]

> Therefore, since we are justified by faith, we have peace with God through our Lord Jesus Christ. [Rom. 5:1]

> And to one who does not work but trusts him who justifies the ungodly, his faith is reckoned as righteousness. [Rom. 4:5]

The biblical nature of the doctrine of justification by faith alone is clear from these and many similar passages. There are, however, a few New Testament texts which seem to conflict with this teaching. One of them is Philippians 2:12. In this instance, however, some of the same principles of interpretation which helped us to understand why James 2:14–26 does not conflict with this great doctrine will show that Philippians 2:12 does not conflict either.

Paul states in Philippians 2:12:

> Therefore, my beloved, as you have always obeyed, so now, not only as in my presence but much more in my absence, work out your own salvation with fear and trembling.

At first glance this passage seems to conflict with what Paul states in Ephesians 2:8–9 and Romans 4:5; 5:1. How can you "work out your own salvation" if salvation/justification is by faith alone? Is it possible that Paul teaches something here which contradicts justification by faith alone? There are at least three powerful reasons why it would be incorrect to interpret this verse as standing in contradiction to what Paul teaches elsewhere concerning the doctrine of justification by faith.

First, our emphasis on the careful analysis of words should cause us to note the meaning of the key word *work out*. (It is a single word in Greek.) This term is different from the one Paul uses when arguing against the belief that we can earn justification by works. In those passages the terms used are the noun *ergon* and the derivative verb *ergazomai*, but here he uses *katergazomai*. This is, of course, clear in the Greek text, but it is also clear in numerous English translations as well, especially those in the King James tradition, which includes not only the King James, but also the English Revised, the American Standard, the Revised Standard, and the New American Standard. The New English Bible and the New International Version also join in and translate *katergazomai* "work out" and not "work for" or "work to get." Unfortunately not all biblical versions translate the Greek term this carefully.

It is critical at this point to observe just how the apostle uses this term elsewhere in his writings. It appears twenty times in the Pauline Letters: Romans 1:27; 2:9; 4:15; 5:3; 7:8, 13, 15, 17, 18, 20; 15:18; 1 Corinthians 5:3; 2 Corinthians 4:17; 5:5; 7:10, 11; 9:11; 12:12; Ephesians 6:13; and Philippians 2:12. It should be noted that in each of these passages there is no idea of meriting or earning something, for the law does not earn wrath (Rom. 4:15), sin does not earn covetousness (Rom. 7:8), nor does generosity earn thanksgiving (2 Cor. 9:11). The way Paul usually uses and understands this term can be seen even more clearly in the following instances:

> For I will not venture to speak of anything except what Christ *has wrought* through me to win obedience from the Gentiles, by word and deed. [Rom. 15:18, italics added]

> The signs of a true apostle *were performed* among you in all patience, with signs and wonders and mighty works. [2 Cor. 12:12, italics added]

It is clear that in these two instances there is no idea of meritorious works in view. There is no concept of earning something. Christ did not ''earn'' obedience from the Gentiles through Paul, nor did Paul earn the ''signs of a true apostle.'' Rather these signs were manifested or demonstrated to the Corinthians. Paul's apostleship was a fact. It was the outworking of that fact and reality which was manifested to the Corinthians. In a similar way Paul is not telling the Philippians to merit or earn their salvation, but rather to manifest (demonstrate or live out) the salvation which they already possess.

Second, we should note the context in which Philippians 2:12 is found. Actually the clause we are discussing, ''work out your own salvation,'' is neither a complete verse nor, more importantly, a complete sentence. In seeking to understand what Paul means here the best commentary is not some other passage in the Bible, but the rest of the sentence. Philippians 2:12–13 is the complete sentence in which the words ''work out your own salvation'' are found.

We note here that verse 13 begins with the word ''for'' (*gar*). This means that the reason for Paul's exhortation in verse 12 is to be found in verse 13. To word this a little differently, the ''for'' of verse 13 reveals that the ground or basis of Philippians 2:12 is the reality spoken of in verse 13. It is because ''God is at work'' in the hearts and lives of the Philippian Christians that Paul tells them to work out their own salvation. It is, in other words, because the Philippian Christians have already been justified/saved (1:28); it is because they are already saints (1:1); it is because they are already "in Christ" (1:1) and are therefore a "new creation" (2 Cor. 5:17); it is because of all this that Paul tells them to live out (manifest, demonstrate, work out) the salvation which they already possess.

The basis of this Pauline exhortation is the reality that the God the Philippians believe in has already transformed them into a new creation. They have through the regenerating work of the Holy Spirit been born again. They have died to sin and have been raised to newness of life (Rom. 6:1–5). The basis of this exhortation to the church, and for that matter the basis of all the commands given to God's people, is the great truth that God has transformed and is transforming them through the Holy Spirit into the image of his Son. This teaching must never be forgotten, for it is a continual theme of Scripture (see, e.g., Rom. 7:5–6; 8:1–4). No wonder Paul has the confidence to say to the Philippians, "And I am sure that he who began a good work in you will bring it to completion at the day of Jesus Christ" (1:6).

Finally, and this could well have been mentioned first, it is the same author who wrote, "By grace you have been saved through faith" (Eph. 2:8), and "Work out your own salvation"! We are not dealing with the teaching of two different authors but rather with the same person. Since the apostle Paul himself argues most forcefully and eloquently that justification is by faith alone, it would appear that for him this cardinal teaching and the meaning of Philippians 2:12 do not conflict. It is true, of course, that at times people are inconsistent, but Paul by any standard was a brilliant theologian. For him to be inconsistent on this crucial point for which he fought so hard is extremely unlikely. (For the evangelical the doctrine of inspiration also argues strongly that Paul's teachings are consistent.) It would seem far more likely, then, that our understanding of the meaning of Philippians 2:12 is incorrect rather than that the apostle has made a major error in his theology at this point.

This is confirmed by a closer look at the whole Book of Philippians. Paul is not writing an evangelistic treatise seeking to show the Philippians how they can be saved/justified. Nor is he endeavoring to defend this doctrine against a misunderstanding by the Judaizers. On the contrary, he is writing to "saints" (1:1) who can "rejoice in the Lord" (3:1). Furthermore, in this very letter Paul teaches clearly that justification does not come out of one's own doing, but comes rather as a gift from God *through faith* (3:9). In light of this it is extremely unlikely that "work out your own salvation" should be interpreted as teaching the very opposite. It is best, then, to interpret our passage as follows, "Since you Philippians have been justified by faith alone and since you have experienced a rebirth by the Holy Spirit, who is continually working in your lives both to change your innermost being to desire his good pleasure and to enable you to carry it out, live out [manifest or demonstrate] with fear and trembling the salvation you possess."

In seeking to understand the meaning of this difficult passage of Scripture we have again found the basic hermeneutical principle discussed in the previous chapter helpful. This principle emphasizes the importance of understanding the meaning of the key building blocks which make up a sentence. In this instance we must understand what the key term *work out* means. To do this we looked first at other writings of the apostle where he uses the same word. Since elsewhere he does not use this term to mean "earn" or "merit" but rather "manifest" and "demonstrate," it probably means the same in this instance as well. Second, and this is the main emphasis of this chapter, we examined the grammatical context in which the term is found. The little word *for* clearly indicates that Paul is not speaking of earning one's salvation: the ground of the command (''for'') is the fact that the Philippians were already the children of God and that God was through his Spirit already working his good pleasure in them.

A third principle which we found helpful in understanding this verse, and which will be the theme of the next chapter, is that we should always seek to understand a passage in the context of what its author says elsewhere. Any teaching of Paul (or of any other author) should be interpreted in light of what Paul (or the other author) teaches elsewhere. Since Paul more than any other writer in the New Testament emphasized that salvation is a matter of grace and comes by faith alone, it is very unlikely that he would be saying the very opposite in this passage. It is highly improbable that Philippians 2:12 conflicts with what Paul teaches elsewhere concerning justification by faith. We shall deal in greater detail with this principle in the next chapter. It might also be pointed out here in passing that Philippians 2:12 reveals a continuity between Paul and James in that Paul also sees a need for one's salvation, which is by grace through faith alone, to be demonstrated and manifested by good works.

What Does It Mean to Be Filled with the Spirit? (Eph. 5:18)

Various passages in the Epistles of the New Testament are troublesome for different reasons. At times we encounter difficulty because an author may assume certain knowledge on the part of his readers which we today do not possess. Two examples of this are Paul's reference to being baptized for the dead (1 Cor. 15:29; see pp. 152–57) and the bodily ailment which caused him to preach the gospel to the Galatians (Gal. 4:13). Unlike the original readers of these letters, who understood exactly to what the apostle was referring, we today do not have access to this information. Another reason why certain passages cause difficulty is the complexity of the subject matter (e.g., predestination) or the apparently contradictory nature of the material (e.g., divine predestination and human responsibility). In a few rare instances the presence of textual variants can cause difficulties as well (Rom. 5:1; Col. 2:2).

On numerous occasions, however, passages are difficult to understand not so much because of the text itself, but because of the popular and erroneous interpretations associated with it. Rather than modify or give up these precious interpretations, we prefer to force the text to fit them. In actuality, however, no biblical text can be forced to fit an interpretation. The text has meant, means, and will always mean exactly what the author consciously willed it to say. As a result we can never force a text to mean what the author did not mean. It means today what the author meant when he wrote it. And this cannot be changed. We can, however, consciously or, more often than not, unconsciously misinterpret the text to fit our own views, but in so doing we do not change the meaning of the text but only place on it an alien meaning.

One example of a text associated with an erroneous understanding is Ephesians 5:18, where Paul states, "And do not get drunk with wine, for that is debauchery; but be filled with the Spirit." A popular interpretation of this passage is that being "filled with the Spirit" refers to an experience which raises a believer to a new stage in the Christian life. Another name given to this supposed experience is the baptism of (or more correctly "in") the Spirit. This experience is seen as enabling the believer to arrive at a new level of discipleship in which God gives to him or her various spiritual gifts such as are mentioned in 1 Corinthians 12:4–11. Usually there is an accompanying sign which verifies that the individual has truly had this experience, and that sign is speaking in tongues.

Although the charismatic movement, in which this theology is so dominant, is a recent phenomenon, the underlying thought has ancient roots. There are similarities with the idea of a "two-level" ethic found in the early church, particularly in the writings of Tertullian and Origen in the second and third centuries. Here we find a two-level view of Christian experience in which certain believers attain only the first level of the Christian life and are concerned with such things as the Ten Commandments, the golden rule, and the love commandment. On the other hand, there is a higher ethic or level, which only certain individuals attain. At this level a person surrenders such things as material possessions, marriage, and family. We can see in such an ethical system the beginnings of a two-level system in which laity and clergy are distinguished.

A far more significant and influential predecessor of this theology is found in the Methodism of John Wesley, who envisioned two distinct levels in the Christian life. Through faith in Jesus one enters the level of justification. Here one is saved, justified, forgiven, and granted eternal life. Subsequently, however, one should seek the second level of sanctification. Although Wesley himself never claimed to have obtained this level of Christian perfection, he preached it. This basic two-stage understanding of the Christian life has spread widely and has had numerous offshoots. We see variations of it when we speak of receiving Jesus as our Savior and then later making him Lord, of having Christ dwell in our hearts but later placing him on the throne of our hearts, of being saved and then later receiving the baptism of/in the Spirit, of being justified and then later being sanctified, of being saved and then later finding some sort of a spiritual secret for the deeper life.

One major problem that has frustrated many of those involved in this kind of theology is how a person can know or prove that he or she has experienced this second blessing or level. What is the sign which verifies that a person has indeed experienced sanctification or, as it is more popularly called, the baptism of/in the Spirit? Some have argued that the sign of this experience is swooning or being slain in the Spirit, that is, fainting because of this second work of the Spirit. Others argue that the sign is a shaking which the Spirit brings on an individual in this experience. Still others argue that the sign is "treeing the devil," that is, chasing the devil out of one's life. In 1901 in Topeka, Kansas, and in 1906 in Los Angeles, there came to the forefront a different sign, which soon became the clear proof of having been baptized in the Spirit. This was the sign of speaking in tongues.

The phenomenal rise and growth of the Pentecostal movement at the beginning of this century and the more recent charismatic movement have brought about the spread of this theology throughout the Christian world. Ephesians 5:18 is seen as an important support of this theology. It is actually a more useful text than the seven passages in the New Testament which refer to the baptism of/in the Spirit (Matt. 3:11; Mark 1:8; Luke 3:16; John 1:33; Acts 1:5; 11:16; 1 Cor. 12:13), for whereas Christians are never commanded to be baptized in the Spirit, they are commanded here to be filled by the Spirit. Yet on closer examination, this text does not fit the charismatic teaching of a two-level Christian experience. This is clear from the grammar in this verse.

The clearest indication that Paul is not commanding the Ephesian Christians to enter into a second level of the Christian experience is the fact that the command is in the present tense. In Greek one uses either the present tense or the aorist tense with the imperative mood, that is, with commands. The present tense generally indicates that the command is to be continually obeyed. This means that Paul is saying in Ephesians 5:18, "Be *continually* filled with the Spirit." It is clear from the tense of this command that Paul is not urging his readers to have an experience once and for all which places them on a new level in the Christian life, but rather to be continually filled with the Spirit. The command therefore does not refer to a one-time experience as in charismatic teaching, but to a continual everyday experience in which Christians are being ruled by the Spirit. Grammatical considerations reveal that Paul's command cannot be interpreted as urging a once-in-a-lifetime experience which will initiate the individual into a second level of the Christian life.

The question of how one is to be continually filled with the Spirit is more difficult to answer. If the participles found in Ephesians 5:19–21 are to be interpreted as instrumental in nature, Paul is explaining in these verses how Christians are to be filled with the Spirit. It is by addressing one another in psalms and hymns and spiritual songs, by singing and making melody to the Lord with all our heart, and by giving thanks always and for everything. Most scholars, however, do not see these participles as being instrumental but as describing the manner in which being filled with the Spirit should be manifested. But how, then, are we to be filled with the Spirit? Most suggestions tend to focus on what the believer must do: we must empty ourselves of all personal ambition, we must "pray through" until God blesses us with his Spirit, we must cleanse ourselves of every sin, and we must dedicate ourselves totally to Christ. Regardless of whether or not there is value in such suggestions, the emphasis is a dangerous one. It focuses on what works we must do in order for God to bless us with his Spirit. It almost gives the impression that we must persuade a reluctant God who does not want to bless us with his Spirit to nevertheless do so. Thus we must talk God into being willing to fill us with his Spirit.

Perhaps two additional Pauline passages concerning the believer's relationship to the Spirit may be of help. In Ephesians 4:30 Paul states, "And do not grieve the Holy Spirit of God, in whom you were sealed for the day of redemption." In a similar manner he declares in 1 Thessalonians 5:19, "Do not quench the Spirit." Is it possible that instead of needing to persuade God to fill us with his Spirit, we need rather to stop hindering (i.e., grieving, quenching) the work that the Spirit is already seeking to do in our lives? Jesus said that God is much more willing to give his Spirit to those who ask than human fathers, who are evil, are willing to give good things to their children (Luke 11:13). It is true that we have for the moment stepped out of the Pauline Epistles, but surely the apostle Paul would agree with Luke that God is eagerly seeking to fill us with his Spirit. If this is true, it may be that instead of concentrating on how we may somehow entice God to fill us with his Spirit, we need to concentrate rather on no longer hindering the work which the Spirit is already seeking to do in our lives. The reason why so many of us are not filled with the Spirit is that we grieve and quench what he is seeking to do in our lives.

How do we grieve and quench the Spirit? It is significant that the command in Ephesians 4:30 is located in the middle of a paragraph of ethical commands. It is unlikely that Ephesians 4:30 was meant to be read in isolation from the other injunctions. It may well be, therefore, that rather than seeking some experience which will automatically fill us with the Spirit, we should put away falsehood, speak truth to each other, refrain from anger and stealing, perform honest work, avoid evil talk, and put away malice (see Eph. 4:25–32).

We possess within the Scriptures the will of God for us; we have his commandments to us. We should not search heaven and earth for some special experience which will automatically fill us with the Spirit. If we keep his commandments, then we shall find that day after day we are filled with his Spirit. Having begun a good work in us, God is eager to bring that work to completion (Phil. 1:6). And he has already given us his Spirit to assist us in this. The God of all grace is not looking for us to perform some mighty act by which we arrive at some second level in the Christian life. He wants us only to stop hindering the work of the Spirit which is already going on in our lives. As we seek by his grace to obey him and keep his commandments, we shall be filled with his presence. On the other hand, just as a parent-child relationship is hindered and grieved by disobedience on the part of the child, so do we by disobedience hinder and grieve the work which the Spirit seeks to accomplish in us.

In Ephesians 5:18 Paul is not urging us to have an experience which will result in what Wesley called sanctification or what charismatics today call the baptism in the Spirit. Rather he is commanding us to be continually filled with the Spirit. This does not refer to a one-time experience but to a continual relationship with the Spirit in which we no longer quench what he is trying to do in our lives. God through his Spirit is already at work in us, seeking to make us desire and do his perfect will. To know his will we need not ascend into heaven to bring Christ down, for the word is close by (Rom. 10:6b–8). Jesus said, "If you love me, you will keep my commandments" (John 14:15). As we trust in the grace of God and keep his commandments, we shall be filled with the Spirit.

Do God's People Not Sin? (1 John 3:6, 9)

In the first letter of John we are confronted with statements which at first glance seem to conflict with both experience and the teachings of the Scriptures elsewhere. In 1 John 3:6 and 9 we read:

> No one who abides in him sins; no one who sins has either seen him or known him. . . . No one born of God commits sin; for God's nature abides in him, and he cannot sin because he is born of God.

The problem raised by these verses is immediately apparent, for believers even in their best moments still sin. Our experience seems to give the lie to what these verses claim. One can, of course, so redefine sin that it may be possible for a Christian not to commit sin as it is newly redefined, but the Bible does not redefine sin in such a manner. A denial of sin in the life of the believer can be built only on a naiveté concerning the magnitude of the problem of sin and depravity in the human heart and a misconception of what has and what has not yet been effected in our redemption. The resurrection of the body is still future, and so is our ultimate deliverance from sin and death. More important, however, the apparent meaning of 1 John 3:6 and 9 conflicts with what the Scriptures teach elsewhere concerning our being justified sinners, but sinners nonetheless. Did not our Lord teach us to pray, "Forgive us our sins, for we ourselves forgive every one who is indebted to us" (Luke 11:4)? Was the apostle Paul simply talking about his preconversion sins when at the end of his life he referred to himself as the "foremost of sinners" (1 Tim. 1:15)? The way the Scriptures speak of sin in the Christian life (see Rom. 14:23; 1 Cor. 6:18; 15:34; James 2:9; 4:17) clearly assumes the presence of sin in the life of the believer.

Even if we were to ignore our experience and the rest of Scripture, 1 John 3:6 and 9 would raise problems with what we find in the rest of this brief letter. There are several instances in which the author refers to sin in the life of the believer. Among the verses in which it is evident that the author believes that Christians sin:

> If we say we have no sin, we deceive ourselves, and the truth is not in us. If we confess our sins, he is faithful and just, and will forgive our sins and cleanse us from all unrighteousness. [1 John 1:8–9]

> My little children, I am writing this to you so that you may not sin; but if any one does sin, we have an advocate with the Father, Jesus Christ the righteous. [1 John 2:1; see also 1:6; 5:16–17; and the exhortations not to sin found in 2:15; 3:11–12]

It is clear from these references that the same author who writes, "No one who abides in him sins," and "No one born of God commits sin," also writes that those who do sin have Jesus Christ as their advocate before God (2:1) and that if they confess these sins, God will in his faithfulness and righteousness forgive them of all their sin (1:9).

Numerous attempts have been made to resolve this problem. One such attempt is to speak of two different kinds of Christians: the one literally does not sin and the other does. First John 3:6 and 9 speak of the former, whereas passages like 1 John 1:8–9 and 2:1 speak of the latter. Such a view is often found in Holiness, Methodist, and Pentecostal literature. According to this view, 1 John 3:6 and 9 are to be interpreted literally, that is, the former group of Christians in fact do not sin. They are referred to as those who have been "sanctified," "baptized in the Holy Spirit," and "filled with the Spirit." They are believers who truly abide in Christ. When, and only when, a Christian has had this second experience are 1 John 3:6 and 9 literally true. (Usually along with such views there is of necessity a redefinition of sin as well.)

Our text, however, gives no hint of a division of Christians into two such classes. Actually verse 6 speaks of all humanity as being divided into two classes. Either one does not sin and thus is abiding in Christ, or one sins and has not seen or known him. It is also clear that the latter group is of the devil (3:8). This would be a rather harsh classification for Christians who are not perfect. Such an explanation, then, is not permitted by our text, for there is no hint anywhere that the author is making some sort of a distinction between two groups of believers. Furthermore, the author's classification of himself as one who confesses his sins (note the "we" in 1 John 1:9) refutes such a view.

Another attempted explanation sees in the word *abides* of 1 John 3:6 the key for understanding these passages. According to this explanation, Christians do not sin when they abide in Christ. When Christ dwells and reigns in them, they do not sin. The problem arises when Christ no longer abides in believers, for then they can and do sin. There are two difficulties with such an interpretation. For one, there is no hint in 1 John that a Christian can pop in and out of an "abiding" state. John does not say "whenever one abides" or "at those times when one abides," but simply speaks of those who abide, that is, those who are in an abiding relationship with Christ. Second, to abide in Christ is explained further in 3:6 as knowing him. To abide in Christ means to know Christ, to be a Christian. It means to keep his commandments (3:24), to confess Jesus as the Son of God (4:15), to abide in love (4:16), and to break bread at communion (John 6:56). Clearly, to abide in Christ refers simply to being a Christian and not to being an élite Christian who possesses a unique holiness.

Other attempts which try to explain our passages state that the author is inconsistent and that what he says here cannot be reconciled with what he says elsewhere, or that our passages must be understood as hyperbolic and as an exaggerated presentation of a desired goal that unfortunately cannot be attained. It should be noted that the author gives us no hint at all concerning the latter view. We should not assume that an author is exaggerating unless there are some clues in the text or in his other teachings that he is doing so. John does not give us the slightest hint that he is using hyperbole in these passages. As to the former explanation, is it likely that the author of 1 John was so illogical that in his own mind he did not reconcile the statements of 1 John 3:6 and 9 with what he says elsewhere? This does not seem very likely.

How then can we explain these passages? At this point the issue of syntax plays a cardinal role. Probably the most helpful procedure is to note carefully the tenses used in these verses. In describing past actions the Greek language has four specific tenses: the aorist, imperfect, perfect, and pluperfect. In general it can be said that the imperfect tense indicates the continual doing of some past action ("They *were driving* for two days"). The perfect indicates an action which took place in the past and has continuing consequences in the present ("They *have been married* for ten years"). The pluperfect indicates an action which took place in the past and had continuing consequences in the past ("They *had been married* for ten years when this happened''). The aorist is the least precise of the four past tenses and is the one normally used to refer to something in the past without emphasizing anything about the past action (''He *saw* an accident''). Unfortunately, in describing present actions there is only one tense available in Greek; and it must serve to describe present actions that are punctiliar in nature (''Jesus *heals* you''), present situations that have continuing consequences (''We *are* God's children''), and present actions that are continually being done (''He *is* always *praising* God'').

In 1 John 3:6 the verb ''sins'' is in the present tense, and in 3:9 ''commits'' is also in the present tense. These can be and probably should be translated as ''continually sins'' and ''continually commits.'' With regard to 3:9 it should be noted that the New American Standard Bible translates this verb as ''practices'' sin, and the New International Version translates it ''will continue to'' sin. The grammar clearly permits this translation, and two important factors argue in its favor. The first is that interpreting the verb as indicating a continual practicing of sin will allow us to harmonize the author's teaching here with what he says elsewhere in the letter concerning the fact that Christians do sin. All things being equal, an interpretation that harmonizes the data should be chosen over one that does not, for writers desire to be consistent in their works. A second and more important syntactical reason for interpreting the verbs in this manner is found in 3:9, where we read ''he cannot sin.'' In Greek this consists of the verb ''to be able'' (*dunatai*) and the present infinitive ''to sin'' (*hamartanein*). In Greek the present infinitive is usually used when a continuing activity is being referred to, whereas the aorist infinitive is used when one does not wish to refer to a continuing action, or when one wishes to refer to a punctiliar action. If John wanted to emphasize that individuals begotten of God are not able to sin *ever*, he would have used the aorist infinitive rather than the present infinitive we find in 3:9. What our passage states is that those who are begotten of God are not able to continue sinning or to abide in sin. By the use of the present infinitive the author reveals that he is not referring to an act of sin but to a practicing of sin. The use of the present participle in 3:6 (*hamartanōn,* "no one who [continually] sins") and 3:8 (*poiōn,* "he who [continually] commits sins") supports this understanding.

The problem encountered in our text is resolved once we understand the grammar, specifically, the tense of the verb, and thus see that John is referring not to acts of sin, but to the continuing practice of sin. As believers we do sin, yet John tells us that although we should not, if we do, we have Jesus Christ as our advocate before God (2:1), and if we confess our sins, God will graciously forgive us (1:9). To live in sin, however, is something else. The person who abides in Christ cannot continue to abide in sin also. To abide continually in sin means that one is associated with the devil, who sinned from the beginning (3:8), rather than with the God of righteousness.

In this short chapter we have looked at some problem passages in the Epistles whose difficulties were resolved by a close examination of their syntax (grammar). Needless to say, we have done so in a superficial manner, for we did not even explain the rules of Greek syntax. To do so would require a much larger and different work. What we have attempted to demonstrate is that, in the interpretative process, just as there is a need to understand correctly what individual words mean, so there is also a need to understand the syntax by which these words are related to one another.

This can, of course, be best done by a careful analysis of the syntax of the Greek New Testament, for the authors wrote in that language. On the other hand, we should also carefully analyze a good translation of the Greek text. We have been richly blessed in our generation with numerous excellent translations of the Bible; perhaps no generation of the English-speaking world other than the sixteenth century has witnessed such a wealth of translations. In translating the Greek text for us, the translators made judicious selection not only of the words which they chose, but also of the grammar. Their selections of tenses, conjunctions, and punctuation were carefully weighed and discussed. They took great care in seeking to represent accurately the words and thoughts of the New Testament writers. To profit most from their efforts, we must look carefully at the words and the syntax they used to express the thoughts of the inspired writers. We need likewise to come to our texts with both reverence and care as we seek to understand the revelation of God found in the New Testament.

3

Understanding the Context
The Author's Writings

In seeking to understand the meanings of terms and the syntax in which they are found, our biggest aid is the context which the author gives them. We have already referred to the hermeneutical circle and the fact that the precise meaning of a word is determined by the meaning of the statement in which it is found, and that the meaning of the statement is of course dependent on the meaning of the word. The meanings of words and statements are also determined by the meaning of the paragraph in which they are found, which in turn is determined by the meaning of the statements, which in turn is determined by the meaning of the words. Fortunately all of this goes on simultaneously and often unconsciously in the mind of the interpreter. Since we are interested in understanding what authors mean by the words and sentences they write, we must study the context in which they write.

The specific context that we shall look at in this chapter is the context of an author's writings. The words in a given writing should always be interpreted in the light of what the author says elsewhere. Unless there is proof to the contrary or a specific statement that the present material is at odds with what was written previously, an author should be granted the premise of being relatively consistent. This should be granted to any author of reasonable intelligence. For thoughtful and careful authors it should be granted even more readily.

In seeking to understand the apostle Paul's statements, then, we should assume that what he says in one setting will be reasonably consistent with what he says elsewhere. Thus if Paul is speaking about the law in one passage, it is helpful to know what he says elsewhere on the same subject. Yet an even greater certainty as to an author's thought can be obtained if we narrow the context. For instance, what Paul says on a subject in 1 Thessalonians will be helpful in understanding what he means when he speaks about the same subject in Romans. But knowing what Paul says elsewhere in Romans on this same subject will be more useful. And what Paul says in the same chapter will be even more useful. And what Paul says in the same paragraph will be still more useful. And what Paul says in the sentences immediately before and after is even more useful than that. And what Paul says in the rest of the sentence is most useful of all!

In this chapter we shall look at several difficult passages in the Epistles and seek to interpret them in light of their authorial context.

Does God Remain Faithful When We Are Faithless? (2 Tim. 2:11–13)

Within the Scriptures we encounter a number of instances where in the midst of a passage we are totally surprised by the way the argument turns. We are anticipating that the argument will proceed in a certain manner when, lo and behold, the author "throws us a curve." An example of this is found in Romans 9, where Paul is talking of God's having loved Jacob and hated Esau (v. 13), of his having mercy on whomever he wills and hardening whomever he wills (v. 18). Then in verse 19 Paul raises the question, "Why does he still find fault? For who can resist his will?" At this point the reader tends to agree with the question and respond, "Yes, Paul, that is a good question. What about this?" The next verse clearly catches the reader by surprise, for instead of proceeding to answer the question he has raised Paul states, "But who are you, a man, to answer back to God?"

Another passage in which the apostle catches us by surprise is the poetic form of 2 Timothy 2:11–13:

> The saying is sure:
>
> [1] If we have died with him, we shall also live with him;
> [2] if we endure, we shall also reign with him;
> [3] if we deny him, he also will deny us;
> [4] if we are faithless, . . .

At this point we expect something like what we have just found in line [3]—"he also will deny us"; but instead we find in line [4] "he remains faithful—for he cannot deny himself." Here we are taken somewhat by surprise, for line [4] seems to deny what line [3] says.

As we compare the first two lines, it is obvious that there is close agreement in both form and content. The subject in both parts of each line is "we," and our doing something positive is said to result in future blessing—we shall live and we shall reign with Christ. The only difference in these two lines is the change in tense from the past "have died" (a culminative aorist) to the present "endure" (a durative present). The third line differs in tense as well, for here we have a future tense "[shall] deny," but the more important difference is one of form. Here, although the subject of the protasis (the subordinate "if" clause) is still "we," the subject of the apodosis (the independent clause) is "he," that is, God. Yet the meaning is still quite close: "if we deny him, we shall be the recipients of God's denial [lit., he will deny us]." In the third line just as in the first two lines what we do results in a corresponding consequence of good or evil. It may well be that the form of the third line has been changed to make it more compatible with the well-known saying of Jesus, "Whoever denies me before men, I also will deny before my Father who is in heaven" (Matt. 10:33). This is probably the reason why line [3] was written as we find it rather than as "if we deny him, we shall also be denied."

The fourth line, however, raises numerous questions and problems. Its form after the protasis is totally different, for in contrast to the first three lines, there is no mention of "we" or "us" in the apodosis or second clause. Even more puzzling than the change in form is the question of the meaning of this line. Is the last clause ("for he cannot deny himself") to be understood as a threat or a promise? We shall address ourselves to this question shortly, but it would be better to deal with the meaning of each statement in order.

After mentioning his own suffering for Christ (vv. 9–10), Paul introduces the hymn of verses 11–13 with a well-known idiom, "The saying is sure." (For other examples see 1 Tim. 1:15; 3:1; 4:9; Titus 3:8.) The first line has frequently been interpreted as referring to a martyr's death. But in view of the parallel in Romans 6:8, where Paul states, "But if we have died with Christ, we believe that we shall also live with him," it would be better to interpret this line as referring to the experience of baptism, which was intimately associated with conversion. The tense of the verb (an aorist) supports this interpretation. The second line, which refers to enduring for Christ, has caused little difficulty. The consequence of reigning with Christ brings to mind such passages as Revelation 5:10; 20:4, 6; and 22:5—"and they shall reign for ever and ever."

The third line speaks of denying Christ. As already mentioned, it is probable that behind this statement lie the words of Jesus in Matthew 10:33. (It is also probable that a parallel to denying Christ is being ashamed of him and his words [Mark 8:38].) It is interesting to note the progression of tenses in the protasis of the first three lines. In line [1] we have a past tense (an aorist) which refers back to the experience of conversion and baptism; in line [2] we have a present tense (a durative present) which refers to a present continual patient endurance for Christ's sake; and in line [3] we have a future tense which refers to a possible future renunciation, denial, or repudiation of our faith. Such questions as to whether a true Christian can ever deny Christ or whether believers will always persevere in their faith are not in the mind of the author. This text is not interested in such speculation. The author in this hymn is simply repeating the words of Jesus that to deny him will result in being denied on the final day of judgment.

This brings us to line [4]. There are two basic ways of interpreting this line. If we interpret it as a continuation of the thought of line [3], we see this line as containing a threat: "If we are unfaithful [in the sense of becoming apostate], God will remain true to his holiness and righteousness and bring upon us his holy wrath and eternal judgment, for God is not able to deny his holy character and nature [lit., himself]." This interpretation has the merit of following the thought pattern of the previous lines. In each of them either good behavior results in good consequences or bad behavior in bad consequences. One logically expects therefore that the bad behavior of line [4] (being unfaithful) will result in a bad consequence. As a result of reading the first three lines, one expects the apodosis of line [4] to be a threat.

On the other hand, there are several problems with this interpretation which suggest that line [4] should be interpreted as a promise rather than a threat. One reason involves the verb which is translated "are faithless" (*apistoumen*). This verb can mean "to be unbelieving" in the sense of not ever having put one's faith in Jesus Christ (see Rom. 3:3; 1 Pet. 2:7; cf. also the noncanonical Mark 16:11). However, the verb can also mean "to be faithless" in the sense that some Christians lack the kind of faith they ought to have. (It is so used in Luke 24:41.) The noun (*apistia*) can also be used in this sense, as in Mark 9:24 where a father cries out to Jesus, "I believe; help my unbelief!" By contrast, in Romans 3:3; 11:20 and 23 it is used to describe the unbelief of non-Christians. It is evident, therefore, that although this verb and its corresponding noun can be used to refer to unbelief in the sense of not ever having placed one's faith in Christ, these terms can also be used to refer to a Christian's lack of trust. The verb "are faithless" can within the norms of language mean to lack saving faith or to lack the kind of faith we as Christians ought to have, that is, to be weak in faith. The former would require that line [4] be interpreted as a threat; the latter would require that it be interpreted as a promise.

A second problem with interpreting line [4] as a threat is in the apodosis "he remains faithful." In the Pauline literature the expression "God is faithful" occurs five other times. In each of these instances we find some positive statement or promise with regard to the issue at hand: "God is faithful, by whom you were called" (1 Cor. 1:9); "God is faithful, and he will not let you be tempted beyond your strength" (1 Cor. 10:13); "He who calls you is faithful" (1 Thess. 5:24). (See also 2 Cor. 1:18; 2 Thess. 3:3; cf. Heb. 10:23; 11:11; and 1 John 1:9.) As a result of the positive contexts in which this expression occurs in the New Testament, and especially in Paul, it seems reasonable to assume that it should be interpreted in a similar manner, that is, as a promise, in 2 Timothy 2:13 as well.

Finally, we need to look at the expression "for he cannot deny himself." Although there is no clear linkage in terminology, this statement calls to mind the words of God when he affirmed his promise to bless Abraham and multiply his seed and swore an oath to this purpose (Gen. 22:16–18). Since there was no one greater than himself to swear by, God swore by himself (Heb. 6:13). When God bestows his gracious promises on his people, he has indeed "sworn and will not change his mind" (Heb. 7:21). The reason for this is evident—God cannot deny himself! He must keep the oath which he has sworn to himself. If this is indeed the way that this expression is to be understood, then line [4] is to be interpreted as a promise rather than a threat.

In light of the above, we should interpret the hymn as progressing in this way:

[1] A statement of reassurance that reminds the readers that when they died with Christ in their conversion, they passed from death into life and shall one day live eternally with Christ;

[2] A promise that patient endurance for Christ in time of tribulation will one day result in our reigning with him eternally;

[3] A solemn warning which recalls the words of Jesus in Matthew 10:33 that the act of denial, which is a repudiation of our faith, will result in the Son of man's repudiating us before the throne of God in the great day of judgment;

[4] A word of comfort and reassurance for sensitive Christians who are burdened with their failures and shortcomings: God's faithfulness is not dependent on the degree of our faithfulness. He will abide faithful to his covenant promises, for he has sworn an oath to this effect; he cannot be untrue to his sovereign promises to us.

It is evident that line [4] was never meant to open the door for possible apostasy. It is not a charter to unfaithfulness. Rather it is meant to serve as consolation for troubled souls. It is meant as a reassuring word that God is faithful to his people far above all that we could ever ask or think. Great indeed is the mercy of our God: "As a father pities his children, so the LORD pities those who fear him" (Ps. 103:13). Even when we prove faithless, he in his grace and mercy remains true to his promises. He has sworn us an oath that he will never fail us nor forsake us (Heb. 13:5). This is "Amazing Grace" indeed! "O the depth of the riches and wisdom and knowledge of God! How unsearchable are his judgments and how inscrutable his ways!" (Rom. 11:33).

Did Paul Learn His Gospel? (Gal. 1:12)

In the opening chapters of Galatians Paul seeks to demonstrate that he is a true apostle in the fullest sense. Apparently his opponents had raised questions with regard to his credentials as an apostle. They claimed that if he was an apostle at all, his apostleship possessed less authority than that of the Jerusalem apostles and that whatever authority he did possess had been given to him by those apostles. To answer his critics Paul points out that he is an apostle "not from men nor through man, but through Jesus Christ and God the Father" (1:1). This was borne out, among other things, by the independent course he took from the beginning (he never went to Jerusalem until three years after his conversion, and then he saw only Peter and James [1:18–19]), and by the fact that when he went to Jerusalem fourteen years later (2:1), the Jerusalem apostles acknowledged his apostolic authority among the Gentiles (2:9) as being equal to Peter's apostolic authority among the Jews (2:7–8).

Another argument Paul uses to prove his apostolic authority is the fact that his gospel came to him directly from God. In Galatians 1:11–12 he states:

> For I would have you know, brethren, that the gospel which was preached by me is not man's gospel. For I did not receive it from man, nor was I taught it, but it came through a revelation of Jesus Christ.

These verses have caused considerable confusion, for elsewhere Paul speaks of having "received" and "delivered" certain traditions, terminology usually used to describe the process of receiving from predecessors various traditions and in turn passing them on to successors. We have a number of examples of this in Paul's letters. In 1 Corinthians 11:23 the words of the Lord's Supper are introduced by Paul with, "For I received from the Lord what I also delivered to you." Likewise in 1 Corinthians 15:3 Paul introduces what is generally recognized as a pre-Pauline christological formula with, "For I delivered to you as of first importance what I also received."

Where and how did Paul "receive" this gospel which he tells the Corinthians he delivered to them (1 Cor. 15:3)? No doubt this took place in much the same manner as the Corinthians "received" it, that is, by learning it from Christian teachers. This appears to be correct in light of the immediate context, where the same term (*paralambanō*) is used to describe how the Corinthians received the gospel: "Now I would remind you, brethren, in what terms I preached to you the gospel, which you received, in which you stand, by which you are saved" (1 Cor. 15:1–2a). If the reception of the gospel by the Corinthians was by the process of teaching and preaching (15:1), then it would appear that Paul's reception of the gospel, which is described by the exact same word (15:3), must have taken place in a like manner. It appears, then, that the term *received* in 15:3 does not refer to a direct divine revelation from heaven, but rather to a mediated delivering of the divine message by Christian teachers.

There are other reasons for believing that Paul in his letters reproduces certain traditions which he had learned from other Christians. These traditions can usually be discerned in Paul's letters by the presence of much un-Pauline vocabulary, an un-Pauline literary style, an atypical (this does not mean contradictory!) theological emphasis, a unique rhythm and balance, or a string of relative clauses. Such clues have led most Pauline scholars today to believe that, among other passages, 1 Corinthians 15:3–7; Philippians 2:6–11; Colossians 1:15–20; Romans 1:3–5; and

3:24–26 witness to early Christian formulations that Paul "received" and incorporated into his letters and preaching.

Besides this reference to Paul's having received certain traditions in the same way that the Corinthians had received them, it is most difficult to assume that the apostle learned nothing about the Christian faith during his career as a persecutor of the church. Certainly as a persecutor Paul must have known something about what Christians believed, for his persecution of the early church was not based on racial or economic considerations but theological ones. Something that Christians were saying and teaching clearly offended him. Obviously, Paul must have known what Christians basically believed and stood for. A dedicated persecutor would seek to know all that he could about the group he was victimizing in order to be better able to refute them.

It is also important to note that Paul acknowledges that three years after his conversion he went up to Jerusalem and spent fifteen days with Peter and James (Gal. 1:18–19). As one commentator has aptly put it, it is quite unlikely that during all this time they talked about nothing but the weather. Surely they must have talked about Jesus and the faith which all of them proclaimed.

It seems clear, therefore, that Paul did acquire considerable information about the Christian faith in a nonsupernatural manner both before and after his conversion. How can we reconcile this with his statement that his gospel did not come from man, that he was not taught it, but that on the contrary it came to him through a revelation of Jesus Christ? While it is true that both before and after his conversion Paul acquired certain facts about the Christian faith, it must be pointed out that the gospel which Paul preached was not simply certain bare facts or information about Jesus. It involved the interpretation of those facts and their theological implications, that is, the kerygmatic interpretation of those facts. It was only through the revelation of Jesus Christ on the road to Damascus that the truthfulness of these facts and their theological implications became known to him. Both the truthfulness of the gospel and some of its major theological implications, as well as his apostolic commission, came to Paul through divine revelation. These were revealed not learned; they came from the Lord not man. It was not through human teaching but through Paul's encounter with Jesus Christ that Pauline theology originated.

All the theological implications of the gospel which were revealed to Paul on the way to Damascus cannot be discussed here, but it may be profitable at this point to mention a few in order to demonstrate why he could say that his gospel came through the revelation of Jesus Christ.

1. One area revealed to Paul on the way to Damascus involved soteriology, or the doctrine of salvation. Paul learned from this revelatory experience that salvation cannot be obtained through the keeping of the law. Even his "blameless" keeping of the law (Phil. 3:6) was useless, for as he learned from his encounter with Jesus Christ, his zeal for the law had made him the very enemy of God! His righteousness melted away when he realized that although he was as a Pharisee blameless according to the law, he was in fact oppressing the people of God. Yet God in his grace saved him. By grace and grace alone God had forgiven him and bestowed on him the very righteousness of Jesus Christ. On the road to Damascus God revealed to him that justification is not of works but by grace alone, and that this justification can be appropriated only by faith.

2. With regard to Christology Paul learned that the one he opposed and ridiculed was indeed alive. The resurrection of Jesus authenticated for Paul all the teachings of Jesus. Jesus of Nazareth was indeed the Christ of God, but he was more than that. In the Old Testament the Voice from heaven was never the voice of a human; it was not even the voice of an angel. It was the voice of God! Yet the one who spoke to Paul was Jesus. Therefore this Jesus must

truly be Lord, the God of the Old Testament. It is not surprising, therefore, that we find in Pauline theology a high Christology indeed. Paul can speak of Jesus' preexistence and lordship over all creation; it is before him that every knee will one day bow and confess that he is both Christ and Lord (Phil. 2:10–11).

3. Concerning eschatology or the doctrine of last things, it was also clear to Paul, as he reflected on his encounter with the risen Christ, that since Jesus had truly been raised from the dead the messianic age had indeed begun. The end of the ages had come (1 Cor. 10:11). The resurrection of the dead had begun. Christ was the firstfruits of the resurrection (1 Cor. 15:23). Another fact that would have given support to this conclusion was the coming of the promised Spirit. The promise of Joel had been realized. The days of the outpouring of the Spirit (Joel 2:28), to which the prophets looked forward, were already present. The presence of the Spirit in the life of the church was the firstfruits of the age to come (Rom. 8:23), the guarantee of our inheritance (Eph. 1:14; see also 2 Cor. 1:22; 5:5). The end times were not simply some far distant hope, for the messianic age had already begun.

There are a number of other theological implications that were revealed to Paul through his encounter with Jesus Christ. One of these would appear to be the doctrine of the church as the body of Christ ("Saul, Saul, why do you persecute me?" [Acts 9:4]). Another is the universal offer of the gospel to both Jew and Greek. Stephen and the Hellenists had hinted at this earlier, and now it was confirmed as true. Stephen's preaching would later be supported by Paul's reflection on the fact that the promised Spirit fell on both Jew and Greek on the basis of faith alone. It is not surprising, therefore, that Paul above all others proclaimed to both Jews and Greeks the great doctrine of justification by faith alone.

There does not seem to be any conflict, therefore, between, on the one hand, Paul's having learned certain things about the Christian faith both from and through men and, on the other hand, his claim that his gospel came supernaturally by the revelation of Jesus Christ. Clearly it was on the road to Damascus that Saul of Tarsus recognized the truth of the Christian message as well as many important theological consequences of the work of Jesus Christ. Here, too, he was commissioned to be the apostle to the Gentiles. All of this did not come through men, nor was he taught it. On the contrary, it came through the divine revelation of Jesus Christ. As a result Paul could say, "For I would have you know, brethren, that the gospel which was preached by me is not man's gospel. For I did not receive it from man, nor was I taught it, but it came through a revelation of Jesus Christ."

Are We to Praise God for All Things? (Rom. 8:28)

One of the favorite Bible verses of the Christian church throughout the centuries has been Romans 8:28. From this text Christians have drawn strength and encouragement in times of deepest despair and gloom. Despite the experience of tragedy, pain, and disappointment, there has come through this verse a word of reassurance and comfort from God. God has not forsaken his children. He has not failed them. No, on the contrary,

> We know that in everything God works for good with those who love him, who are called according to his purpose.

Yet despite the blessing that this statement has been in the history of the church, what Paul is actually saying has frequently been misunderstood. Some people unfortunately have read into this verse some strange and unchristian concepts. A certain woman who had not been feeling well was hospitalized, certain tests were made, and the resulting diagnosis was cancer. It was an extremely malignant form of cancer, and the prognosis was bleak. She had in fact but a few months to live. The shock was great, and she wept a great deal, not so much for herself but for her family. She was afraid for her husband and children because she felt they needed her. A friend from church visited her during this time of grief and turmoil. After the usual chitchat, the friend said, "Let's thank God for your cancer." The supposed grounds for such a suggestion were texts like 1 Thessalonians 5:16 ("Rejoice always"), Philippians 4:4 ("Rejoice in the Lord always"), and Romans 8:28 (see also Eph. 5:20 and 1 Thess. 5:18). The dying woman's friend believed that Romans 8:28 teaches that all things which happen to a Christian are good, and therefore we should praise God for everything that occurs.

Apart from the question of whether this approach is therapeutic or wise in counseling people experiencing such grief, the real issue is the soundness of the theology underlying such a view. For those familiar with philosophy, the friend's reasoning sounds very much like Greek Stoicism, a philosophy founded by Zeno. It received its name from Zeno's teaching his ideas in the Painted Porch (i.e., the Stoa) of Athens. Stoicism is essentially pantheistic in that it believes that God permeates all things. He is the rational, active cause of all. Hence, the Stoics argued as follows: God is in all things; God is reason; therefore, all things that happen are ultimately reasonable. The Stoics believed that all things that occur are to be accepted as essentially good. As a result, in times of distress and disappointment they found courage in their belief that all things are good; acceptance of this truth brought comfort and peace to them. Many Christians have unknowingly interpreted Paul's theology in Romans 8:28 in the context of a Stoic framework.

But does Paul teach that all things are good or that for Christians all things that take place are good? A number of considerations oppose such a position. One difficulty with this view is that it ignores the problem of sin. This is not the best of all possible worlds. In the opening chapters of

Genesis we read that one of the results of sin is that the creation is under a curse (Gen. 3:17–19). Paul speaks of this in the immediate context of Romans 8:28:

> For the creation waits with eager longing for the revealing of the sons of God; for the creation was subjected to futility, . . . the creation itself will be set free from its bondage to decay and obtain the glorious liberty of the children of God. We know that the whole creation has been groaning in travail together until now; and not only the creation, but we ourselves, who have the first fruits of the Spirit, groan inwardly as we wait for adoption as sons, the redemption of our bodies. [Rom. 8:19–23]

Disease and death are part of the curse under which the present world groans. This is why the believer prays constantly for the time when the creation will be renewed beyond its original perfection, when God will wipe away all tears, and when death and sin will be no more. Thus we pray, "Thy kingdom come" (Matt. 6:10), and "Our Lord, come!" (1 Cor. 16:22). When disease and death befall a believer, they cannot be good. To praise God for cancer, therefore, is to praise him for what is evil and a curse. To praise God *while* we have cancer is indeed appropriate, for because of his nature and deeds God is worthy of praise; but to praise him *for* cancer is to praise him for evil, and this is far from appropriate.

It should also be noted that Romans 8:28 is beset with several textual and exegetical difficulties. The textual problem involves the question of whether "God" is the subject of the verb *works*. In three extremely important Greek manuscripts (Codices Vaticanus and Alexandrinus and the Chester Beatty Papyrus) "God" is the subject. While it is true that the majority of the Greek manuscripts do not have "God" as the subject, it should be remembered that most of them originated many centuries later. If the reading *God* is followed, the exegetical difficulties disappear for the most part, for Paul is not saying that all things work together for our good, but rather that God is at work in all things (good or evil) for our good. On the other hand, if the majority text, which does not have "God" as the subject, is followed, the subject of the verb *works* is unclear. The difficulty of this particular reading is an argument in favor of the majority reading. (A basic rule in textual studies is that the more difficult reading is probably the original one; the less difficult presumably reflects an editor's attempt to clarify.) In this case the two most likely possibilities are that the verse is to be interpreted, "He [i.e., God] works all things for good," or "All things [the Greek allows this word to be either the subject or the object of the verb] work together for good."

The various English translations reveal this uncertainty. The King James Version reads, "All things work together for good." On the other hand, the modern translations all have God as the subject of the verb:

RSV—"We know that in everything God works for good."

NIV—"And we know that in all things God works for the good."

NASB—"And we know that God causes all things to work together for good."

NEB—"and in everything, as we know, he co-operates for good."

Now it is true that the modern translations include a notation to the effect that "other ancient authorities read 'in everything he works for good,' or 'everything works for good'" (RSV), but these are seen as less likely to be correct.

It is a wise hermeneutical principle not to build theological systems on disputed texts, for the likelihood of any interpretation's being correct can never rise above the combined probabilities of each part. In our text this means that if there is a 50 percent probability that Paul did not write "God" as the subject of the verb *works*, and if the linguistic probability that "all things" is the subject rather than the object of the verb is also 50 percent, then the probability that "all things work together for good" is the correct translation is only 25 percent. (The percentages given are, of course, purely hypothetical.)

The textual and exegetical problems associated with this verse should guard us against building too great a theological structure on it. And when we add to the textual and exegetical uncertainty the Christian understanding of the fall, sin, and the curse on creation, it becomes clear that we should not try to build on this passage the idea that all things that befall believers are good and worthy of praise. It should also be noted that no matter how we translate Romans 8:28, the reason or ground for the Christian assurance found in it is given in verses 29 and 30. Here we read nothing about all things being good, but we read rather about the goodness of God who chose (i.e., "foreknew"), predestined, called, justified, and glorified his children. Surely what Paul is saying is that the God who chose, predestined, called, justified, and glorified his children is present and working with us in all circumstances (whether they are good or evil), seeking our good. Because of this we can truly be thankful.

How should a Christian respond to the tragedies of life and to the command to "rejoice always"? With regard to the latter we should note that not only did the apostle Paul write this command, but he also wrote, "Rejoice with those who rejoice, weep with those who weep" (Rom. 12:15). We find that even our Lord wept with others over the death of his friend Lazarus (John 11:35). That the dominant disposition of the Christian should be one of rejoicing and praise goes without saying. Our sins have been forgiven (Rom. 4:7); we have God as our Father (Rom. 8:15); we have the assurance of life everlasting (John 3:16, 36); and our Lord has risen from the dead and ever lives to beseech the Father on our behalf (Heb. 7:25). We already have the firstfruits and guarantee of our salvation, the Holy Spirit (2 Cor. 1:22), and this assures us that God, having begun a good work in us, will one day bring it to completion (Phil. 1:6). We have the assurance that our Lord will never fail us nor forsake us (Heb. 13:5), and that he will be with us until the end of history (Matt. 28:20). How can the Christian not be joyous and full of praise in the light of all this? Yet we still groan inwardly as we await the consummation of all things, and there are even times when we are actually commanded to weep and share the grief of others, even as we are to rejoice and share in their joy (Rom. 12:15).

As to the tragedies in life, we must remember that the wickedness of the human race, death, and disease are evils brought about by the fall. These cannot be called ''good.'' This is evident from the fact that before the fall they did not exist, and in the world to come they will not exist either. To call these good or to praise God for them is to insult the character of a holy and just God. To say that Auschwitz, Treblinka, and Sobibor; cancer, Parkinson's disease, and AIDS; and death itself are good, and to praise God for them cannot but cause us to wonder what kind of a God is being envisioned. Is this the God who loves the world and gave his only Son for its redemption? It is hard to see any great similarity.

How, then, should Christians respond to tragedy and pain? Can we praise God in Auschwitz? Can we rejoice when dying of cancer or when experiencing the death of someone greatly loved? Yes, *in* Auschwitz the believer can still praise God, but not *for* Auschwitz, for it was one of the greatest evils that sinful humans have ever created. What it stood for is forever condemned. Yet in Auschwitz the believer can still rejoice that even amid the most evil attempts to create hell on earth, God will never leave nor forsake. The most that evil persons can do is to take away our physical life, but they can never alter the fact that we are headed for a place which has eternal foundations whose builder and maker is God (Heb. 11:10). Even in

Auschwitz the believer is assured that tribulation, distress, persecution, famine, nakedness, peril, or the gas chamber can never separate one from the love of God in Christ Jesus (Rom. 8:35). Even there we can praise heaven that God is at work shaping and molding us to be more like Jesus, and in the light of eternity this is what really counts.

Similarly, we do not thank God for cancer. We do know, however, that in heaven there is no cancer. This result of the curse will be removed forever. So then, if we experience cancer, we can rejoice that this momentary affliction will one day give way to an eternity of bliss in the presence of Jesus. In a sense we can even rejoice that we will see our Lord sooner than will others, and that "to die is gain" (Phil. 1:21).

In Romans 8:28 Paul was reminding the Roman Christians, who loved God and were called according to his divine purpose, that God is present with his children and works with them in all circumstances. Elsewhere Paul also assured his readers that God would not permit them to suffer or be tempted above what they were able to bear (1 Cor. 10:13). These words of the apostle are still valid today. If the time comes in which we must take up the cross of suffering, we need to remember that even here (indeed, above all here) God is at work in and for us. And it may very well be, as saints have found throughout the centuries, that in such circumstances we shall experience the presence and grace of God as never before.

Is Every Government from God? (Rom. 13:1–7)

Another passage that has caused ongoing problems in the history of the church is Romans 13:1–7. Here Paul states:

> Let every person be subject to the governing authorities. For there is no authority except from God, and those that exist have been instituted by God. Therefore he who resists

> the authorities resists what God has appointed, and those who resist will incur judgment. For rulers are not a terror to good conduct, but to bad. Would you have no fear of him who is in authority? Then do what is good, and you will receive his approval, for he is God's servant for your good. But if you do wrong, be afraid, for he does not bear the sword in vain; he is the servant of God to execute his wrath on the wrongdoer. Therefore one must be subject, not only to avoid God's wrath but also for the sake of conscience. For the same reason you also pay taxes, for the authorities are ministers of God, attending to this very thing. Pay all of them their dues, taxes to whom taxes are due, revenue to whom revenue is due, respect to whom respect is due, honor to whom honor is due.

We become uneasy with this apparent blanket commendation of all governments when we recall how the Nazi regime (and others like it) used this passage in the 1930s and 1940s to promote loyalty and support for itself and its policies from both Protestants and Catholics.

It is not surprising, therefore, that through the centuries Christians have struggled with this passage and how it applies to their immediate situations. Already Origen (185–254) raised the question of whether a power which persecuted the church, fought against the faith, and destroyed religion was truly of God. In the sixteenth century the Reformers took a number of positions on how this passage was to be interpreted. For John Calvin any resistance to lawfully constituted authority was damnable, and not even a persecuting and unbelieving ruler could be forcibly resisted. Christians had no defense against a corrupt government other than prayer and flight, but if commanded by such a government to do what God forbids, they would have to disobey and remain true to God. On the other hand, the Magdeburg Confession, written by Lutherans fighting for their faith against a Roman Catholic emperor, saw it as a positive duty to resist all attacks against the true religion—their Lutheran faith. John Knox, a disciple of Calvin, went still further and claimed that it was the duty of a believer to rebel and seek the overthrow of idolatrous princes.

In seeking to understand the teaching of our text it is important to distinguish two questions: What did Paul mean by Romans 13:1–7? and what is the present-day significance of what Paul meant? It is clear that what the text means is that the Roman Christians who received this letter in A.D. 56 should obey their Roman leaders and give them the respect and taxes which were their due. Our text, then, is very much like Mark 12:13–17; 1 Peter 2:17–19; 1 Timothy 2:1–2; and Titus 3:1 in this regard. The reason behind Paul's admonition is that all authority comes ultimately from God and that rulers are servants of God for their people's good. (Here Paul is also in agreement with such Jewish writings as Wisdom 6:1–3 and Josephus *History of the Jewish War* 2.140.) We should remember that for the most part Nero had been a good emperor up to this time, that Roman law and justice had a positive effect on society, and that the government had frequently come to the defense of the church. The last-mentioned fact is evident from such incidents as are recorded in Acts 16:35–39 and 18:12–16, and there is no reason to think that situations like those we find in Acts 21:31–36; 22:22–29; 23:16–35; and 25:6–12, which took place after Paul wrote Romans, did not occur earlier as well. The *pax Romana* was also most conducive to the spread of the gospel throughout the world, since travel everywhere within the Roman Empire was now safer and more rapid.

On the other hand, Paul was not naive about the Roman government. After all, its leaders were unregenerate, and his writing of Romans 8:35 ("Who shall separate us from the love of Christ? Shall tribulation, or distress, or persecution . . . or sword?") indicates that he was well aware of a negative role that government could play. When Paul wrote Romans, however, he was not concerned with hypothetical possibilities or exceptions to the rule. He could write as he did because the Roman government functioned within the guidelines which he gives in our passage. Rome had not yet asked the church to give to Caesar the things that were God's. There might well come a time when the words of Peter must be heeded—"we must obey God rather than men" (Acts 5:29)—but this was not yet a significant problem. The Roman government of A.D. 56 was far from perfect, but it was nevertheless an instrument of God in support of peace and justice instead of chaos. In general those who did evil were punished and those who did right were, if not always praised, at least left alone. This was far better than a situation in which "every man did what was right in his own eyes" (Judg. 21:25). Paul may also have believed it important to emphasize this need for obedience because in A.D. 49 there had been a serious clash in Rome between believing and unbelieving Jews. As a result, Emperor Claudius had expelled all the Jews from Rome (Acts 18:2). Concerning this event Suetonius wrote around A.D. 120, "Since the Jews constantly made disturbances at the instigation of Chrestus [this is undoubtedly an error and should be read "*Christ*us"], he [Claudius] expelled them from Rome" (*Lives of the Caesars* 25).

The main problem Christians face in our passage is not so much the meaning of the text, but rather the significance of that meaning for today. It is understandable why Paul would have commanded the Roman Christians to obey their government in A.D. 56, but the abuse of this text in Nazi Germany and in other totalitarian systems makes us most uneasy, for Paul seems to be giving a blanket blessing on all governments. Yet clearly there are times when we cannot give Caesar what he asks, for example, when he asks for that which belongs to God alone. Furthermore, it is surely incorrect to assume that Paul naively thought that all governments were legitimate. The Roman government of A.D. 56 was, but he was well aware of evil governments in the history of Israel. He knew of many rulers of Israel and Judah who did evil in the sight of the Lord. He was not unaware of such evil rulers as Ahab, Jeroboam, Joash,

Zechariah, and Pekah, as well as Sennacherib and Antiochus Epiphanes. Furthermore, he had even warned of the coming of the Antichrist (see 2 Thess. 2:1–12). As a result, he knew of instances where to obey the government would have been to deny God. He was also well aware of the Roman involvement in the crucifixion of his Lord.

It is often overlooked that Paul in discussing the need to obey authority because of its being ordained of God describes that authority. The authority that he envisions as ordained of God is "not a terror to good conduct, but to bad" (Rom. 13:3). It is an authority which gives its approval to those who do good (v. 3). It is an authority which is "God's servant for your good" and which executes God's "wrath on the wrongdoer" (v. 4). This is how Paul describes governments which possess God's divine approval and which Christians are to obey. In general, Rome in A.D. 56 met this description. It is likewise clear that numerous governments such as Nazi Germany do not. To expect Paul, however, to be concerned with teaching when one must disobey government would clearly be wrong. The need at hand, in light of A.D. 49 and other events of which we are perhaps not aware, was to emphasize the Christians' duty to obey and not rebel against the legitimate authority of Rome.

In my own experience this text became relevant and significant when in the 1970s I was being urged to protest against the Vietnam War by not paying my taxes or at least by not paying the portion of my taxes which went for the military budget. In wrestling with this passage I asked myself several questions: In general does my government punish evil and reward good? Did the Roman government of A.D. 56 use the taxes it collected for nonsocial purposes? Did Rome use the tax moneys of believers for its militaristic aims? Does my government demand for itself that which rightly belongs to God alone? and, finally, Was the Roman government which Paul commanded his readers to obey a better government than mine? After answering yes to the first three questions and no to the last two, it became clear that if the Roman Christians were to obey the Roman government of A.D. 56 and pay it the taxes due, how much more ought I do the same with regard to my government! In light of the meaning of the text in A.D. 56 its significance for my own situation in the 1970s became quite clear. Other areas of protest were still available, but nonpayment of taxes seemed to be excluded by the text.

The time may come, of course, when in our own country the state turns against the people of God. It did not take long for the "Hosanna" of Palm Sunday to change to the "Crucify him" of Good Friday. God's people were persecuted in Old Testament times by outside powers (Assyria, Babylon, Syria, etc.) and from within as well (various rulers of Israel and Judah). The church has also experienced persecution from without as well as from within. To say that this can never happen in our own country is to ignore both the teachings of Scripture and the lessons of history. If the time ever comes when our government in general rewards evil and punishes good, and when it demands for itself what only God is entitled to, then we shall have to say boldly and clearly, "We must obey God rather than men." But this was not the situation in Paul's day when he wrote Romans 13:1–7, and it is not the situation in which we find ourselves today.

Did Paul's Theology Develop?
(1 Thess. 4:13–18)

In discussions of Pauline theology it is not uncommon to read about the development of Paul's thought. That Paul's theology developed in one sense is certainly true. Surely his theology at the end of his life was not identical with his theology ten minutes after his conversion. Over the years God granted Paul additional revelation (2 Cor. 12:7), and as he reflected on the gospel which God had revealed to him, met with Peter and the other disciples, and studied the Old Testament Scriptures, he must have gained additional insights. There is a sense, therefore, in which Paul's theology did indeed develop.

What most scholars mean when they talk about development in Paul's theology, however, is something quite different. Many insist that Paul's theology changed over the course of years, so that what he taught in his early letters (such as 1 Thessalonians) he no longer accepted in his later ones (such as Romans or Colossians). (Most scholars who hold this view do not accept the Pauline authorship of 1 and 2 Timothy and Titus.) Paul is supposed to have changed his view on such things as the resurrection and the parousia. With regard to the former, Paul's original view of a merely physical resurrection to take place at the parousia (1 Thess. 4:13–18) changed to a more spiritual view of a resurrection (1 Cor. 15:35–50) which takes place at death (2 Cor. 5:1–3). With regard to the parousia Paul supposedly changed from the view that Jesus would return in Paul's own lifetime (1 Thess. 4:15, 17) to the view that the second coming would not take place in his lifetime (Phil. 1:19–26).

Probably the one passage that has most often been cited as proof that Paul changed his view as to the time of the parousia is 1 Thessalonians 4:13–18. Here Paul seems to be teaching that Jesus would return in Paul's lifetime:

> For this we declare to you by the word of the Lord, that we who are alive, who are left until the coming of the Lord, shall not precede those who have fallen asleep. [v. 15]

Such a view as to the time of the parousia was clearly incorrect, so Paul later changed and taught that the parousia would not come in his own lifetime. Sometimes a major crisis such as Paul's facing death (2 Cor. 1:8–9) is suggested as having caused this change.

The basic question involves whether Paul did in fact teach at one time that the parousia would take place in his own lifetime. This is not the same as asking whether Paul personally believed at one time that he would be alive when Jesus returned. Paul may very well have believed that he would be alive, yet never have taught this in his letters. We have no access into Paul's mind as to what he may have believed but not taught. As a result, we must narrow the question to, Did Paul ever assert in his letters that the parousia would take place in his lifetime? Since the passage most often cited as proof that he did is 1 Thessalonians 4:15, 17, we can reword our question as follows: Does Paul teach in 1 Thessalonians 4:15, 17, that Jesus would return in the apostle's own lifetime? For some people the fact that Jesus did not return in Paul's lifetime is proof that he did not teach this. Such reverence for the Scriptures and their infallibility is praiseworthy in one sense, but in another sense such a view places one's own doctrinal presuppositions above the meaning of the biblical text itself. As one who holds the view that the Bible is the only infallible rule of faith and practice, I believe that we must let the text speak for itself. We cannot tell the text what it can or cannot say. True reverence for the Word of God is to listen to it. Rather than predetermining what 1 Thessalonians 4:15, 17, can or cannot mean, we must reverently seek to understand what Paul meant by this text.

There are a number of philosophical and historical objections that could be raised against the view that Paul's theology developed (in the sense of "changed") between his earlier and later writings. These are helpful and will be examined later, but priority must always be given to the text itself. The immediate context of 1 Thessalonians 4:15, 17, involves the fact that certain Thessalonian Christians have died since Paul founded the church there. From Timothy Paul has heard (probably in Corinth) that some of the Thessalonians are troubled over the fate of those who have died since Paul's departure. Will they miss out on the "blessed hope, the appearing of the glory of our great God and Savior Jesus Christ" (Titus 2:13)? Paul seeks to assure the Thessalonians that they will not. He does not want his readers to be ignorant and as a result grieve like non-believers who have no hope (1 Thess. 4:13), so he declares to them that those who have died in Christ will rise from the dead to meet the returning Jesus. They will therefore not miss out in any way on sharing the glory of the parousia. Then "we who are alive, who are left until the coming of the Lord... shall be caught up together with them ... and so... always be with the Lord" (vv. 15, 17). Paul then applies this great theological truth to the situation in Thessalonica: "Therefore comfort one another with these words" (v. 18). The Thessalonians need not grieve over those who have died in Christ. They can take comfort in the fact that the dead in Christ as well as the living will share in the glorious event of the parousia.

Does Paul, however, teach in verses 15 and 17 ("we who are alive") that he would personally be alive at the parousia? There are several considerations that should caution us before we answer this question affirmatively. For one, it should be noted that what Paul is primarily emphasizing in 1 Thessalonians 4:13–18 is not that he and the recipients of this letter will be alive when Jesus returns. Rather, he is affirming that the dead in Christ will not miss out on the parousia. Accordingly, Paul does not bother to clarify who among those presently living will be alive at the parousia and who will not. Since the contrast lies between those Thessalonians who are dead in Christ and those who are alive, where else can Paul include himself and the recipients of this letter except with those who are alive?

Second, the economy of language used did not permit Paul to clarify the various possibilities that faced him and the Thessalonians. If, simply for the sake of argument, we assume that Paul believed that not all the recipients of this letter would be alive at the parousia (and certainly it is extremely doubtful that Paul believed that no more Thessalonian Christians would die before the Lord returned), how would Paul have worded it? The following by its very nature would have been overly clumsy: "We who are alive, who are left until the coming of the Lord (although, of course, some of us presently alive may not be alive then, but may have joined those who are asleep), shall not precede those who have fallen asleep." Since Paul was primarily concerned with teaching about the dead in Christ, such exactness about the living was unnecessary. A simple deduction on the part of the Thessalonian Christians would have enabled them to add this qualification to Paul's words.

Third, a literal interpretation of Paul's words in 1 Thessalonians 4:15, 17, which claims that Paul taught that he would be alive at the parousia, requires that Paul also taught that all the Thessalonians living at the time of his writing would likewise be alive at the parousia, for the "we" includes them as well. Few scholars, however, would be willing to go this far. It would be absurd to glean from this passage the idea that whereas in the past certain Thessalonian Christians had died, no more of them would die, but they, along with Paul, would remain alive until the parousia. Such an interpretation is necessitated, however, by reading into the "we" of these verses the idea that Paul is affirming that he would be alive at the parousia.

Fourth, it should be noted that the "we" in verse 15 is qualified by the phrase "who are alive, who are left until the coming of the Lord," and in verse 17 by "who are alive, who are left." If Paul were affirming confidently that he and at least the majority of the Thessalonian Christians would be alive at the parousia, why does Paul add this qualification? Why does he not simply say, "We shall not precede" (v. 15) and "We shall be caught up" (v. 17)? Even if we were to say that adding "who are alive" was natural to show a contrast between the living and the dead in Christ, why does Paul add "who are left until the coming of the Lord" in verse 15 and "who are left" in verse 17? It seems reasonable to conclude that Paul by these additions was indicating that he was uncertain as to whether he and the recipients of his letter would be left when the Lord returned, so he qualified the "we" in this manner.

Finally, it should be noted that in 1 Thessalonians 5:10 Paul uses "we" to describe both those who are awake (i.e., living) at the time of the Lord's return and those who are asleep. The fact that Paul does not say, "so that we who are awake and those who are asleep," but rather, "so that whether we wake or sleep," indicates that Paul is not claiming in 1 Thessalonians 4:15, 17, that he will be alive at the parousia.

It would appear, then, that the context as well as the wording of the text does not require us to interpret these verses as an affirmation by Paul that he would be alive at the parousia. On the contrary, it appears that Paul was well aware that he and the Thessalonian Christians might also be asleep at the parousia. Nevertheless, awake or asleep (1 Thess. 5:10) they would not miss out on the parousia but would meet the Lord and live forever with him.

This interpretation is reinforced by several other considerations as well. One of these involves the occasional nature of Paul's letters. We have already alluded to this when we discussed what Paul was seeking to teach in this passage. We should always be careful in drawing out of the text conclusions on issues that the author is not specifically addressing. It is clear that Paul is not seeking in 1 Thessalonians 4:15, 17, to make a statement about who will be alive at the return of the Lord, but rather about the relationship of the dead in Christ to the parousia. We should therefore be careful not to draw any unwarranted conclusions about Paul's relationship to the parousia.

Second, we should note the date of this letter. First Thessalonians was written some sixteen years after Paul's conversion. In 2 Corinthians 11:23 Paul writes that he was often near death. No doubt some of these instances took place in the years before he wrote 1 Thessalonians. Are we to assume that Paul never thought that any one of these episodes could spell his death? Are we to assume that during his stoning at Lystra (Acts 14:19–20) Paul thought that it was impossible for him to die because the parousia had not come? This seems highly unlikely.

Finally, we must remember that Paul was well aware that numerous Christians had died in the Lord. On what basis could he conclude that despite having faced death a number of times he would somehow be excluded from death and would survive until the parousia? If it is suggested that Paul may have believed that God had revealed this to him, we must point out that nowhere does Paul mention or appeal to such a revelation.

Did Paul's theological understanding of the parousia develop? Surely he grew richer in knowledge. No doubt Paul at the end of his life had a greater understanding of the parousia and the implications of this event than he did in his earliest days as a Christian. But did Paul's understanding of the parousia change in the sense that he denied what he once affirmed or affirmed what he once denied? And in particular, did Paul affirm in his earliest letters that he would be alive at the parousia and then deny this later? From our investigation of 1 Thessalonians 4:15, 17, we conclude that there is no reason why these verses need to be interpreted as teaching this. On the contrary, within the text there are a number of reasons for denying that Paul sought to affirm that he would be alive at the time of the parousia. We have no way of knowing what Paul may have personally thought on the issue, but it is clear that in this passage, he does not teach that he would survive until the parousia.

Was Paul a Universalist? (Col. 1:15–20)

Within the New Testament several passages have been called hymns because of their rhythmic balance. One such passage is Colossians 1:15–20:

> He is the image of the invisible God, the first-born of all creation; for in him all things were created, in heaven and

> on earth, visible and invisible, whether thrones or dominions or principalities or authorities—all things were created through him and for him. He is before all things, and in him all things hold together.
>
> He is the head of the body, the church; he is the beginning, the first-born from the dead, that in everything he might be pre-eminent. For in him all the fulness of God was pleased to dwell, and through him to reconcile to himself all things, whether on earth or in heaven, making peace by the blood of his cross.

Although this passage raises a number of issues, the particular issue to be dealt with in this section involves the apparent reconciliation of ''all things, whether on earth or in heaven,'' which has resulted by the death of Christ. Does Paul teach in this passage that everyone and everything will ultimately be reconciled to God irrespective of whether individuals accept or reject Jesus Christ in this life? In other words, does our passage teach the universal salvation of all creation?

Such a view while attractive would seem to oppose numerous clear statements in Paul and in the rest of the New Testament. The traditional position of the Christian church on this matter has been that the destiny of each individual will be determined by whether one places personal faith in Jesus Christ during this lifetime. The result will be either eternal bliss (heaven) or eternal damnation (hell). Evangelical Christians do not hold this view because they desire the eternal damnation of non-Christians. On the contrary, many would love to be universalists in this regard, for they are not eager to believe that friends and relatives whom they love will experience the eternal condemnation of a holy and righteous God. If they could vote on this issue, they would gladly vote a universalist ballot. Theology, however, is not determined by vote! The theological reality of an eternal judgment (or of no eternal judgment) is not determined by ballot. God is not an elected official of a democracy; he is the sovereign King.

Theology therefore does not conduct Gallup Polls of what people believe or want to believe, but seeks to discover what the sovereign God has decreed. Theology ultimately is determined by the exegesis of God's revelation, that is, our understanding of the Bible. Our wishes and desires are ultimately irrelevant.

The reason why the statement concerning the reconciliation of all things in Colossians 1:20 raises problems is that elsewhere in Scripture we come across numerous passages which clearly teach that those who reject in this life the love of God in Christ will experience an eternal judgment. The wicked in their judgment are seen as existing in an unchangeable state of torment (Luke 16:26); Jesus portrays the separation of the goats from the sheep as an "eternal punishment" (Matt. 25:46); the fires of hell are described by Jesus as unquenchable (Mark 9:43, 48) and eternal (Matt. 18:8); and the torment of the wicked is seen as continuing "for ever and ever" (Rev. 14:11). Paul also teaches in his writings that the judgment of God involves eternal felicity for the believer, but eternal wrath for the unbeliever. Concerning those who do not obey the gospel he states, "They shall suffer the punishment of eternal destruction and exclusion from the presence of the Lord and from the glory of his might" (2 Thess. 1:9). He also tells the Thessalonians, "For God has not destined us for wrath, but to obtain salvation through our Lord Jesus Christ" (1 Thess. 5:9). (See also 2 Thess. 2:10, 12; Phil. 3:19; Rom. 2:6–10, 12; 5:9.)

In seeking to understand Paul's meaning, we should interpret Colossians 1:20 in the context of his other teachings. Hypothetically, Paul could have changed his views when he wrote Colossians or he could have been inconsistent, but we should assume, unless it is proven otherwise, that a theologian of his stature would be consistent and not make contradictory statements. For the evangelical Christian the doctrine of inspiration and infallibility also argues strongly for consistency in Paul's writings.

One way of understanding Colossians 1:20 which is consistent with Paul's teaching elsewhere involves the meaning of the term *reconcile* in this verse. This term can be understood in light of what Paul says in Colossians 2:15: Jesus has disarmed the principalities and powers and triumphed over them. It is evident from this verse that there exist a serious hostility and animosity between God and all things. The reconciliation of the hostile powers in Colossians 1:20 refers, then, not to a willing rapprochement, but to a reluctant submission such as we read of in 1 Corinthians 15:28 and Philippians 2:10–11. This reconciliation stands in synonymous parallelism with the phrase "making peace." Now peace can be joyously accepted, but it can also be forcibly imposed! Is the peace referred to in our verse the kind of peace that comes when the God of peace crushes Satan under our feet (Rom. 16:20)? The *pax Romana* which existed in the Mediterranean world of Paul's day was of this type. It came through force of arms. But it was peace.

If the reconciliation spoken of in Colossians 1:20 is interpreted in light of Jesus' triumph over the principalities and powers of Colossians 2:15, we should not see this final pacification as a joyous, happy turning to God in faith. More likely we have portrayed here the victory of Christ over his enemies: the powers submit against their wills, bow their knees, and confess with gnashing teeth that Jesus Christ is Lord (Phil. 2:10–11). This forcible subjugation, furthermore, need not involve an eternal state but rather the reconciliation that will take place in the great day when everyone gives glory to God and confesses, willingly or unwillingly, that Jesus Christ is indeed Lord of all. After this the final separation of the sheep and the goats will take place.

A second way of interpreting Colossians 1:20 (it should be pointed out that these two ways are not mutually exclusive but may very well be complementary) is to take into consideration the hymnlike nature of Colossians 1:15–20.

In general, hymns should be interpreted somewhat differently from nonpoetic material. A good example of this is found in Judges 4 and 5. In chapter 4 we have a narrative account of the defeat of Sisera by the forces of Israel led by Deborah and Barak. It is written in prose and should be interpreted literally. On the other hand, we find in chapter 5 a poetic version of the same event. Here we must take into consideration the poetic form and allow for a certain degree of hyperbole and exaggeration, for poetry frequently makes use of these elements to get its point across. It is not surprising, therefore, that in Judges 5 we read that "the earth trembled, and the heavens dropped" (v. 4), "the mountains quaked" (v. 5), and "from heaven fought the stars, from their courses they fought against Sisera" (v. 20). And with regard to an even more familiar incident we have Israel's crossing of the Red Sea described both in narrative and in poetry (Exod. 14 and 15). In the poetic version we read, for example, "the horse and his rider [the Lord] has thrown into the sea" (15:1), "Pharaoh's chariots and his host he cast into the sea" (v. 4), and "thy fury . . . consumes them like stubble" (v. 7).

Even today it is not unusual to find exaggeration and hyperbole present in the songs and hymns of the church. Note, for example, the following verse from Charles Wesley's "Hark! the Herald Angels Sing":

> Hail, the heav'n-born Prince of Peace!
> Hail, the Sun of Righteousness!
> Light and life *to all* He brings [not "offers" but "brings"],
> Ris'n with healing in His wings.

Consider also Isaac Watt's "Joy to the World!":

> He rules the world with truth and grace,
> And makes the nations prove
> The glories of His righteousness,
> And wonders of His love.

The latter hymn if sung in a Russian gulag would be a confession of faith in the sovereignty of God and his future judgment and rule of the world, but it would also be clearly hyperbolic with respect to the present situation. Yet in hymns and poetry such language does not bother us because we accept the presence of hyperbole, for rhyme and meter often put unique demands on the writer, and the genre itself encourages the use of exaggeration for expression. In this regard we even speak of poetic license.

Is it possible that in a similar way the poetic hymn of Colossians 1:15–20 may be using exaggeration and hyperbolic language because of its rhythmic structure? It is noteworthy that the expression *ta panta* (or "all things") is used four times in this passage, and that other forms of this Greek word occur four more times. The balance of the poetic form should also be noted:

> "all things were created *through him* and for *him*" (v. 16b)
> "and *through him* to reconcile to *him*self all things" (v. 20a)

Recently one writer has demonstrated that there exist in both Jewish and Greek literature a number of creation statements in which the term *all* appears with unusual frequency. This tendency and the attempt to balance verse 20 with verse 16 may well have led the hymnwriter to practice the same kind of poetic license that the writers of Judges 5 and Exodus 15, as well as later hymnwriters and poets, found necessary for their works.

If Colossians 1:15–20 is understood in the way we have suggested, this passage does not conflict with what Paul and the rest of the Scriptures teach elsewhere, for what we have here is not a confession in prose using literal terminology, but rather a joyous song celebrating the creative and redemptive work of Jesus Christ who is Lord of all.

If We Are Already Dead to Sin, Why the Exhortation? (Rom. 8:9–13)

Within the Pauline Letters we encounter a number of statements and exhortations which, although standing side by side, appear to conflict with each other. One such example is in Romans 8:9–11 and 12–13:

> But you are not in the flesh, you are in the Spirit, if in fact the Spirit of God dwells in you. Any one who does not have the Spirit of Christ does not belong to him. But if Christ is in you, although your bodies are dead because of sin, your spirits are alive because of righteousness. If the Spirit of him who raised Jesus from the dead dwells in you, he who raised Christ Jesus from the dead will give life to your mortal bodies also through his Spirit which dwells in you.

> So then, brethren, we are debtors, not to the flesh, to live according to the flesh—for if you live according to the flesh you will die, but if by the Spirit you put to death the deeds of the body you will live.

Another example of apparent conflict is found in Colossians 3:3 and verses 2 and 5, where Paul's statement, "For you have died, and your life is hid with Christ in God," is preceded by "Set your minds on things that are above, not on things that are on earth," and followed by "Put to death therefore what is earthly in you: fornication, impurity, passion, evil desire, and covetousness, which is idolatry."

The problem raised by these passages and others like them is that the statements made by the apostle in Romans 8:9–11 and Colossians 3:3 seem to conflict with the exhortations found in Romans 8:12–13 and Colossians 3:2 and 5. If Christians are not in the flesh but in the Spirit, why should they be exhorted and warned not to live in the flesh? If believers have died with Christ, why are they commanded to put to death what they have already died to? Or to use the language of Romans 6, why does Paul tell the Christian who was crucified with Christ and has died to sin (vv. 6, 11, 14) not to let sin reign within (vv. 12–13)? How can a person dead to sin commit sin? In Pauline studies this problem is known as the problem of the indicative (the statements) and the imperative (the exhortations). The issue is by no means a minor one, for many additional passages contain this seeming conflict (see Rom. 6:17–18 and 19; 1 Cor. 5:7b and 7a; 6:11 and 9–10; 10:13 and 12; Gal. 5:25a and 25b; Col. 3:1a and 1b; 3:9b–10 and 9a).

Numerous attempts have been made to resolve this problem. One such attempt explains the problem as arising from a conflict between the Pauline ideal, the apostle's conviction that under the impulse of the Spirit the Christian can be nothing but moral (the indicative), and the reality, which caused Paul to give commands (the imperative) to those who failed to live up to this ideal. Another explanation sees Paul as teaching two separate and irreconcilable ethical systems. The one involves a law ethic and is witnessed to by the imperatives; the other is the ethic of the justified believer and is witnessed to by the indicatives. Unfortunately the apostle never brought them into harmony, so that a basic contradiction stands between the indicative and the imperative. A third explanation argues that there is no real connection or relationship between Paul's theology (the indicative) and his ethics (the imperative). They are simply isolated and separate categories in Paul's thinking which he never reconciled. Still another explanation is to see Paul's teaching as inherently paradoxical; accordingly, we should not try to reconcile the indicative and the imperative, but rather should delight in their dialectical antagonism. One advocate of this view argues that Paul taught that believers should "become [in fact] what they are [in principle]." A final explanation argues that Paul overstates and exaggerates the indicative aspect of the Christian's redemption in order to emphasize that Jesus has brought about a radical break with the old life. As a result, the indicatives should not be taken at face value.

Each of these explanations suggests that the problem between the indicative and the imperative in Paul cannot be resolved, and that an irreconcilable contradiction of some sort is present in this material. Yet before we come to such a conclusion, it may be profitable to look at the biblical data. We should note that the indicatives and the imperatives causing our problem are not found in widely scattered portions of the Pauline Letters. On the contrary, they are intimately associated together. In fact they are frequently found in the same passage. It is therefore unlikely that Paul was unaware of the problem or that he has given in the same sentence two totally different and contrasting theories of Christian ethics. It would appear that at least in Paul's mind the indicative and the imperative were interconnected, belonged together, and made sense.

We should also note that the imperative rests on the indicative and that the order is not reversible. In other words the exhortations of the apostle are based on the reality of the statements. The exhortations do not bring about the truths stated in the indicatives but are built on the reality of the indicatives. We are not exhorted to put the sin in us to death in order to die with Christ. On the contrary, it is because we have died with Christ that we are told to put to death the deeds of the body, that is, sin in us. We are not commanded not to let sin reign in our mortal bodies in order to die to sin. Quite the reverse—it is because we have died to sin that we are told not to let sin reign in our mortal bodies. It is only because Christians have died to sin that they are able to resist it. It is important in this regard to note such words as "so then" in Romans 8:12, "therefore" in Colossians 3:5, "if" in Colossians 3:1, "for" in Colossians 3:3, and "as" in 1 Corinthians 5:7. These passages indicate that the imperative is based and built on the reality of the indicative.

We should note further that there is no textual evidence which suggests that Paul believed that the indicatives were overstatements of some kind. On the contrary, he truly believed that Christians have died, been buried, and been raised with Christ. Probably the key to understanding Paul's teaching here (as well as when he speaks of being in Christ or in Adam and when he depicts the church as the body of Christ) can be found in the concept of corporate solidarity. According to this concept an individual can be so associated with a group or another individual that what is said of the one can also be said of the other. So when Achan sinned (Josh 7:1), it could be said that all "Israel has sinned" (7:11–12). Note also the solidarity between the people who came out of Egypt and their descendants in Joshua 24:6–7, where the writer speaks of the present generation, most of whom were not alive at the time, as having been delivered out of Egypt. In the New Testament we read that if "one member [of the church] suffers, all suffer together; if one member is honored, all rejoice together" (1 Cor. 12:26). In a similar manner, because we are in Adam we experience death through our association with him, yet because we are in Christ we experience life through our association with him.

The apostle sees the church as united to Christ by faith in such a way that what Christ has experienced has also been experienced by the members of his body. Because Christ died, so have they. Because Christ rose, so have they. For Paul this is not some sort of fiction but an actual reality. Believers, because they are in Christ, can be said to have died to sin and been raised with Christ. Viewed from the perspective of the believers' unity with Christ, all these realities, even if not yet fully realized, are theirs. Because Paul views believers from the perspective of all that they are in Christ, he is able to say what he does in his indicatives. Viewing Christians from the perspective of all that they are in Christ involves not just where they are at the moment, but what they have been, are, and will be; and as a result the indicatives are absolutely true. Believers in Christ are not only forgiven, saved, and justified, but glorified, rendered dead to sin, and raised in newness of life. While it may be true that at the present they do not possess all of their inheritance in Christ, all these blessings are theirs nonetheless. In the light of eternity all these are true of Christians. There are no ifs. Believers can be accurately described as forgiven in Christ, saved, justified, glorified, rendered dead to sin, and raised in newness of life. In the indicatives Paul views Christians from the perspective of eternity, which involves a "not yet" dimension, and not simply from the momentary situation in which they now exist.

On the other hand, the imperatives view and deal with Christians in light of their present situation, that is, the "already now." The imperatives deal with what believers have presently realized and where they are at the moment. They view the Christian on this side of the second coming where sin is still a reality and the resurrection still future. The indicatives deal with believers from the viewpoint of what they are in the light of eternity. It is because of what we are in Christ eternally that Paul makes his indicative statements. It is because of what we are in time and on this side of the second coming that he exhorts us to set our minds on the things that are above and not to let sin rule over us.

A story concerning one of the kings of England well illustrates our point. While he was a boy and his father was still alive, he was, of course, the heir to the throne. He was not yet the king, but he would be on his father's death. Accordingly, the boy's tutor would time and time again exhort him with the words, "You are the king, and kings do not behave that way." Now, of course, he was not yet the king, but he was the future king, so he was exhorted to live in light of all he was and would be. Paul in a similar way reminds Christians that they must view their lives in light of all that they are in Christ, and this involves not just the present time but eternity itself. In light of eternity (not yet) and in light of our kingly inheritance already received (now), Paul exhorts us to live like the kings we really are.

Should the Church Hand an Offending Member Over to Satan? (1 Cor. 5:1–5)

Discipline is not a favorite subject in the Christian church today. In evangelical settings there is much interest in following the apostolic teaching and preaching, but there is considerable uneasiness in following the apostles in their practice of church discipline. This is often most difficult to carry out and rightly so, for we do not always possess the clarity of insight that the apostles possessed in their practice of church discipline. Furthermore, we are constantly aware that we need to take heed to ourselves (Gal. 6:1) and be careful that we not fall (1 Cor. 10:12).

Church discipline, however, should not be understood as an act of judgmental vengeance but rather as an act of love for God, his church, and the individual. The command to "judge not" (Matt. 7:1) warns against being judgmental in nature, that is, being critical of others with the aim of hurting them or of making us feel better by making others look worse. Yet to neglect church discipline is to deny the keys with which the church has been entrusted (cf. Matt. 18:18 with what precedes). It is interesting to note in this respect that some of the Reformers, especially Ulrich Zwingli and the Anabaptists, saw the marks of a true church as being not only the true preaching of the Word of God and the right administration of the sacraments, but also the faithful exercise of church discipline.

One of the most troubling passages in the New Testament which deal with church discipline is in 1 Corinthians 5. Paul has heard, perhaps from Chloe's messengers (1:11), about an example of gross immorality in the church. A member of the church was living sexually with his stepmother ("his father's wife"). Such behavior was prohibited in the Old Testament (Lev. 18:8; 20:11), and marriage between a man and his stepmother was also forbidden by Roman law. This is why Paul states that this immorality is "of a kind that is not found even among pagans" (1 Cor. 5:1). It seems that whereas the man himself was a Christian, for the church was directed to take action against him, his stepmother was not, for no church discipline was to be exercised toward her.

After a brief rebuke of the church for its overly high opinion of itself, Paul states in verses 3–5:

> For though absent in body I am present in spirit, and as if present, I have already pronounced judgment in the name of the Lord Jesus on the man who has done such a thing. When you are assembled, and my spirit is present, with the power of our Lord Jesus, you are to deliver this man to Satan for the destruction of the flesh, that his spirit may be saved in the day of the Lord Jesus.

Paul, even though not in Corinth at the time, feels compelled to judge this particular matter, since the Corinthians, who ought to have disciplined the man, have not done so. Although Paul is not physically present, he is nonetheless present in spirit (cf. Col. 2:5), and so he passes judgment. Clearly Paul sees the need for discipline in this matter. It is to the shame of the Corinthians that he had to write them and command them to take action. They should have done so on their own.

A number of questions arise with regard to what the phrase "in the name of the Lord Jesus" modifies. Does it go with "assembled"? With "deliver"? With "pronounced judgment"? Or does it go with "has done such a thing"? The last-mentioned may not be as farfetched as it first appears, for the man may have claimed that his action demonstrated that he was free in Christ and no longer under the law. The New International Version (NIV) favors "assembled in the name of the Lord Jesus," while the Revised Standard Version (RSV) favors "pronounced judgment in the name of the Lord Jesus." We cannot be certain, but in light of the fact that Paul usually associates this particular phrase with a finite verb rather than a participle, the RSV reading should be favored (in the original Greek the word translated "pronounced judgment" is a finite verb, while the word translated "assembled" is a participle; cf. 1 Cor. 6:11; Phil. 2:10; Col. 3:17; 2 Thess. 3:6; but note Eph. 5:20). Another question involves the phrase "with the power of our Lord Jesus." Does it go with "assembled" or "deliver"? The NIV and the RSV both favor "assembled" in this instance, the RSV reading, "When you are assembled . . . with the power of our Lord Jesus."

In verse 5 we come across additional difficult questions which affect our understanding of this passage even more. What does "deliver this man to Satan" mean? What does "for the destruction of the flesh" mean? Finally, what does "that his spirit may be saved" mean? With regard to the last two phrases the RSV reproduces the ambiguity of the Greek text better, while the NIV has eliminated much of the ambiguity and chosen a particular interpretation ("so that the sinful nature may be destroyed and his spirit saved on the day of the Lord").

What does Paul mean by "deliver this man to Satan"? He seems to be referring to expulsion from the church (note v. 2). Although we should not read into the text later doctrines of excommunication, we have here a command to expel the offender from the fellowship of the church. Since this means that the man will leave the fellowship of God's people, where God rules, and be forced out into the world, where the devil rules (Eph. 2:2–3; 2 Cor. 4:4; John 12:31; 16:11), he is in effect to be handed over to Satan. Expelled from the community of God's people, the offender is to be delivered to the realm where the ruler of this age works in those who are disobedient (Eph. 2:2; cf. Col. 1:13).

The offender is to be handed over to Satan "for the destruction of the flesh." This has been interpreted to mean "for the mortification or putting to death of his sinful lusts." This is how Origen interpreted the expression and is the preferred reading in the NIV. Romans 8:13 is seen by some as expressing the same idea, but there Paul speaks of putting to death the "deeds of the body" and not the "flesh." Colossians 3:5, which refers to putting to death evil desires, is likewise not an exact parallel. According to the alleged parallels, one is to put to death evil deeds or desires, but not the flesh. Furthermore, these commands are given to Christians in good standing, not to one about to be expelled from the Christian community for gross sin. The question can also be raised at this point whether Paul really thought that destruction of the flesh or sinful nature can be achieved in this life. Finally, it should be noted that Paul never uses the term flesh (*sarx*) elsewhere in 1 Corinthians to refer to sinful lusts, so that it does not appear likely that he would use it in this way here (see 1 Cor. 1:26, 29; 6:16; 7:28; 10:18; 15:39, 50).

A second possible interpretation holds that Paul is referring to physical suffering. Some scholars see a parallel in 1 Corinthians 11:30–32, where Paul explains that some of the congregation are sick and some have even died as a result of improprieties at the Lord's Supper. It is hoped that through such suffering repentance will result and the offenders will be restored to fellowship. We note, however, that this passage is referring to members *within* the Christian community, whereas the offender in 1 Corinthians 5 is expelled from and stands *outside* the Christian community.

A third explanation is that the destruction of the flesh refers to physical death. Being handed over to Satan means to be handed over to death. Some see death in this case as remedial, that is, through death the offender would atone for his sins, while others see it as purely punitive. The idea that death has some sort of atoning significance is found in rabbinic literature, but it is absent from the New Testament. It seems best to interpret "the destruction of the flesh" as referring to physical illness and even death that the offender will face outside the community of faith.

With regard to the clause "that his spirit may be saved," it should be noted that the word *his* does not appear in the Greek text. Literally Paul states, "in order that *the* spirit [or *the* Spirit] might be saved." The basic issue here is whether Paul sees the discipline of the church as being primarily remedial and for the sake of the offender (in order that *his* spirit may be saved in the final day), or whether he sees such discipline as being purificatory and for the sake of the church (in order that *the* Spirit's presence may remain unhindered, i.e., unquenched, until the final day). In favor of the latter interpretation are the lack of any reference to repentance in our passage and Paul's evident concern for purity within the community (see v. 13). We have a similar example in Ananias and Sapphira, who died for their sin (Acts 5:1–11). Their death was punitive and perhaps purificatory but certainly not remedial, for there was no opportunity for repentance. There are a number of arguments, however, in favor of the former interpretation. One is the use of the term *saved*, which seems far more appropriate for the human soul than for the Holy Spirit. How is the Holy Spirit "saved"? Furthermore, Paul uses the term *spirit* in verses 3 and 4 to refer to his own spirit rather than to the Holy Spirit. It is more likely, then, that he is referring to the human spirit in verse 5 than to the Holy Spirit.

Another passage that helps us determine whether Paul envisions discipline here as remedial or purificatory is 1 Timothy 1:20, where Paul speaks of having "delivered [Hymenaeus and Alexander] to Satan that they may learn not to blaspheme." Once again we find the same terminology ("delivering [someone] to Satan") followed by a statement of purpose ("that they may learn not to blaspheme"). Although the verb "learn" (*paideuthōsin*) can refer to punishment, in the New Testament it is almost always positive in nature. Even when it is used in reference to chastisement, the hoped-for result is positive. In 1 Timothy 1:20 the main reason for delivering Hymenaeus and Alexander to Satan may be punitive and purificatory, but there is also in view a hoped-for repentance as well. Only through repentance and restoration to the community will the expressed purpose that they learn not to blaspheme be fulfilled. If the discipline is merely punitive, how will they learn this? Certainly the ruler of this age will not teach them not to blaspheme. On the contrary, they will be all the more free to do so. Only if there is the possibility of repentance and restoration to the community can the offenders learn not to blaspheme.

Although there may be difficulties and ambiguities with certain aspects of Paul's teaching in our passage, this should not blind us to what we can clearly know and understand. Paul did believe and teach that in certain cases (such as the immorality described in 1 Cor. 5) members of the Christian community were to be expelled (lit., "delivered to Satan"). During this period, since they were no longer within the protected community, they were more liable to experience physical trials (see 1 Cor. 11:30) and even death (lit., "the destruction of the flesh"). Furthermore, such discipline was concerned not only for the community and its relationship with God, but also for the offender. His salvation (lit., "so that the spirit may be saved") was also in view. In the light of this and other passages the church today should clearly rethink its attitude of indifference toward church discipline. If we love God, we must exercise discipline within the church, for he has commanded us to do so; if we love the church, we must be concerned for its purity; and if we love the offender, we must be concerned for his eternal soul.

Is Paul's Teaching on the Law Consistent?

One of the most important and yet confusing areas in the writings of the apostle Paul is his teaching on the law. Despite the vast amount of effort that has been put into the study of this area of Pauline theology, no consensus exists. Not only does Paul use this term to designate different entities, but at times he appears to say contradictory things about the law. It is important to note that the term "law" (*nomos*) possesses a range of meanings in Paul's writings. It can refer to the Ten Commandments ("if the law had not said, 'You shall not covet,'" Rom. 7:7), to the Pentateuch ("the law and the prophets," Rom. 3:21), or even to the whole Old Testament (note 1 Cor. 14:21, where "in the law it is written" is followed by a quotation from Isa. 28:11–12; see also Rom. 3:19 with the quotations that precede it). The term can refer to a principle ("I find it to be a law that when I want to do right, evil lies close at hand," Rom. 7:21) and perhaps to Roman civil law (Rom. 7:1–3), and can serve as a synonym for "works of the law" (cf. Gal. 3:10 and 11), which refers to the keeping of the law in order to gain or retain one's salvation. That the term *law* has a broad semantic range in Paul should not surprise us and should keep us from trying to assign a single meaning to the term wherever it appears in his writings.

In addition to the problem of multiple meanings, there are a number of places in Paul's letters where he seems to be saying contradictory things about the law. One scholar in fact claims that there are five major contradictions. Before investigating two of the areas in which Paul supposedly contradicts himself, it may be wise to reflect for a moment on what we think of Paul's capability as a theologian. It is, of course, possible that Paul did in fact say contradictory things about the law. Yet it is also possible that Paul was an extremely logical thinker. If this is the case (and, if anything, we have grossly understated the apostle's intellectual ability), then he certainly would have seen the contradictions and rectified them, especially since some of the supposed contradictions are found not only in the same letters, but even within the same sections and arguments. We should, then, attribute to the apostle a reasonable degree of intelligence and try to make sense of his various statements concerning the law. It may be that a single harmonious understanding may result. On the other hand, Paul's teachings on the law may "defy attempts at harmonization," as one scholar has claimed; but we should, out of courtesy to Paul, at least make an attempt to see if the supposed inconsistency lies with him or is a result of our own misinterpretation.

One of the areas where a contradiction is said to exist is in Paul's opinion of the value of the law. In a number of places Paul clearly states that the law is good: "So the law is holy, and the commandment is holy and just and good" (Rom. 7:12); "we know that the law is spiritual" (Rom. 7:14; see also Rom. 3:31; 7:7, 13, 16; Gal. 3:21; 5:14). For Paul the law was always the "law of God" (Rom. 7:22). Such statements are not at all surprising from a man who was raised as a Pharisee (Phil. 3:5). Since the law ultimately comes from God, what else can it be but good?

Yet Paul does appear to say a number of negative things about the law as well. In Galatians 3:13 he speaks of the "curse of the law." Indeed, "cursed be every one who does not abide by all things written in the book of the law, and do them" (Gal. 3:10, quoting Deut. 27:26). Our inability to keep the law perfectly brings a curse on us. The law brings universal condemnation, for it comprises a series of "Thou shalt nots," which we all have in fact broken. So for those seeking to establish their standing before God by works of the law there is nothing but condemnation, for any attempt to attain righteousness must meet the requirement of perfect obedience to the commands of the law, which no one can achieve (see also James 2:10). The problem, however, does not lie with the law, but rather with us as human beings. Whereas the law is spiritual, "I am carnal, sold under sin" (Rom. 7:14). With the mind I can approve the law and even desire at times to keep it, but "with my flesh I serve the 'law' [i.e., the rule] of sin" (Rom. 7:25). The law, weakened by our flesh (Rom. 8:3), is not able to make us righteous. It can prescribe what we should do, but it does not contain within itself the power to bring about what it prescribes.

Nevertheless, the law serves a positive function in all this. When Paul talks about the curse of the law, he is not contradicting what he has said elsewhere about the law's being good. The law serves a positive function here in that through it we become aware of our sin (Rom. 3:20; see also

Rom. 4:15; 5:13, 20). The law reveals to us our condition of sin: "if it had not been for the law, I should not have known sin" (Rom. 7:7). For some people this means that Paul views the law as essentially condemnatory, a supposed conflict with what he says elsewhere about the law's being good. Yet is an X-ray machine good or evil when it reveals that the patient has cancer and requires radical surgery for healing? In a similar way, is the law evil because it reveals the cancer of our sin and the need for radical surgery by the Great Physician?

The perfection of the law cannot help revealing our imperfections, and in so doing it serves a good and positive function. It drives those who desire spiritual health, that is, righteousness, to seek, as a gracious gift from God, the righteousness which comes through faith in Christ. Since the law reveals to sensitive people the inadequacy of their own attempts to keep the law, it serves positively by pointing to God's way of righteousness, which is through faith in Christ. Therefore, instead of seeking to create our own righteousness, which cannot help falling short (Rom. 3:23), we joyously submit to the righteousness of God which is in Christ Jesus (contrast Rom. 10:3). Because the law serves as a kind of X-ray machine which reveals our desperate need of God's remedy, it functions positively; it is good in that it leads us to seek the gift of justification which comes through faith in Christ (Eph. 2:8).

A second area in which scholars see a contradiction in Paul's teaching concerning the law involves the relationship between the keeping of the law and justification. On the one hand, Paul states that "no human being will be justified in his [God's] sight by works of the law" (Rom. 3:20); that "a man is not justified by works of the law" (Gal. 2:16); and that "if justification were through the law, then Christ died to no purpose" (Gal. 2:21; see also Gal. 3:11, 23–25; Rom. 4:15). On the other hand, the apostle also seems to argue that justification and its opposite, condemnation, are based on whether or not one keeps the law. One such passage is Romans 2:13–15:

> For it is not the hearers of the law who are righteous before God, but the doers of the law who will be justified. When[ever] Gentiles who have not the law do by nature what the law requires, they are a law to themselves. . . . Their conscience also bears witness and their conflicting thoughts accuse or perhaps excuse them.

It should be noted that in the middle part of this quotation Paul is not saying that the Gentiles do in fact keep the law, but rather that "whenever" or "on those occasions when" some Gentiles keep or do the law, they reveal a knowledge of God's law written on their hearts. The use of the present subjunctive "do" (*poiōsin*) with "when[ever]" (*hotan*) reveals that Paul is referring to occasional acts of keeping the law, and that these occasional instances of obedience to what the law teaches in no way disprove that the Gentiles in question are nonetheless sinners in need of the grace of God. We cannot read this statement without noting what Paul has just said about the condition of the Gentiles in Romans 1:18–32. What Paul is saying is that the Gentiles are not without a witness to God's law and that their occasional keeping of the law reveals that they possess within them some knowledge of the will of God. In the day of reckoning they will be judged according to this knowledge.

With regard to the statement that it is the doers of the law who will be justified (Rom. 2:13), we must remember that this remark is made in the context of establishing that Jews are as much in need of the grace of God in Christ as are Gentiles. Jews, to be sure, possess the law of God, but possession is not enough. One must keep the law of God, for not the hearers of the law but the doers of the law will be justified. But who are the doers of the law? Surely we are to think here of those whom Paul describes in Romans 8—those who are in Christ, who are justified by faith and walk according to the Spirit. There is no conflict, then, between Romans 2:13–15 and what Paul says elsewhere about the law.

Still another passage which is frequently seen as conflicting with the Pauline doctrine of justification by faith is Romans 2:26–27:

> So, if a man who is uncircumcised keeps the precepts of the law, will not his uncircumcision be regarded as circumcision? Then those who are physically uncircumcised but keep the law will condemn you who have the written code and circumcision but break the law.

Again we should note that this passage appears in the section of Romans (2:1–3:19) in which Paul is arguing that the Jew, just like the Gentile, stands in need of justification by faith. In this diatribe against a hypothetical Jewish opponent Paul argues that simply being the physical offspring of Abraham is not enough. Circumcision and possession of the law are insufficient. We must do what the law demands. Breaking the law makes one's circumcision irrelevant (Rom. 2:25). On the other hand, if someone who is uncircumcised, that is, a Gentile, keeps the law, he is in God's sight circumcised in the true sense, that is, one of God's covenant people. A true Jew is not one who is externally or physically a Jew, but one who is a Jew internally (2:29), that is, he is circumcised in heart and possesses the faith of Abraham (Gal. 3:7–9). What, however, does it mean to keep the law? In Galatians 3:10 the implication is clear that no one keeps the law perfectly. How, then, can Paul speak of the Gentiles' keeping the law? Do we not have a contradiction here?

There is a sense in which Paul claims both that no one keeps the law and that the believer does in fact keep the law. With regard to keeping the law perfectly in every respect, Paul clearly teaches that "all have sinned and fall short" (Rom. 3:23). In the sense of absolute obedience to the law, "None is righteous, no, not one; . . . All have turned aside, . . . no one does good, not even one'' (Rom. 3:10, 12). Yet there is a sense in which Paul speaks of the Christian's keeping the law. To trust in Jesus Christ and walk in the Spirit is to keep the law. In so living, the just requirements which the law demands are fulfilled in us (Rom. 8:4), for believers love their neighbors and thus fulfil the law (Rom. 13:8). Through being loving servants to one another we fulfil the whole law, which says, ''You shall love your neighbor as yourself'' (Gal. 5:13–14). The believer who has become a new creature in Christ and is filled with the Spirit can truly love God and neighbor as the law teaches.

Paul makes a clear distinction between the keeping of the law as a believer and the keeping of the law as an attempt to gain a right standing before God. Seen legalistically as a means of achieving salvation or as a means of remaining in a saved state, the law can only condemn. For anyone who tries to establish a relationship with God on the basis of keeping the law there is nothing but condemnation, for ''cursed be every one who does not abide by *all things* written in the book of the law, and do them'' (Gal. 3:10, italics added). Paul agrees with James that ''whoever keeps the whole law but fails in one point has become guilty of all of it'' (James 2:10). Seeking one's own righteousness by keeping the law can lead only to failure, for no one abides by and does all the things written in the book of the law. It can also, because of pride in a false sense of self-achievement, lead to a hardness of heart which refuses to submit to the only way to true righteousness—the righteousness of God which comes through faith in Christ (Rom. 10:3).

The Old Testament law never taught such a legalistic self-righteousness. The law was given in grace to a people already redeemed from their bondage, and it contained provision for sins. The law was given to the covenant people of God who had been delivered out of their bondage in Egypt. The law, furthermore, not only revealed the sovereign will of the holy God, but it led the devout believer in times of failure to seek the grace of God by the sacrificial system and ultimately in the Lamb of God who would take away the sins of the world. But for those who misunderstand the law and seek to establish their standing before God on the basis of their own works of the law, it can only condemn. Paul's argument in Romans and Galatians is not directed against the Old Testament law properly understood, but rather against a misunderstanding of it and a use for which it was never intended—as a legal code through which one earns righteousness and places God in one's debt (Rom. 4:4–5). Paul was not an antinomian; he was not opposed to the law or the commandments of God. Rather, it was his view that as believers walk in the Spirit they keep the commandments of God. Through the Spirit not only do they keep the commandments externally, but they do so with a renewed heart. In this way their righteousness exceeds that of the scribes and Pharisees (Matt. 5:20).

Perhaps nowhere does Paul teach about the Christian's relationship to the law and its requirements more clearly than in Romans 8. "There is therefore now no condemnation for those who are in Christ Jesus" (v. 1) is a favorite verse for many Christians. Yet it is frequently quoted with no regard for its context. In verse 2 Paul gives the reason for the absence of condemnation. Note that he does not say it is because we are justified by faith. Rather he states, "For the law of the Spirit of life in Christ Jesus has set me free from the law of sin and death." There are numerous exegetical questions surrounding this verse; one of the most important involves the referent of the word *law*. We do not need to resolve this issue here, but we do need to note that the absence of condemnation in verse 1 is based or grounded on the freedom achieved by the "law of the Spirit" referred to in verse 2. This in turn is grounded or based on the fact that "God has done what the law

. . . could not do . . . he condemned sin in the flesh, in order that the just requirement of the law might be fulfilled in us, who walk not according to the flesh but according to the Spirit'' (vv. 3–4). Ultimately the absence of condemnation spoken of in verse 1 is grounded on the fact that the Christian, who walks according to the Spirit, fulfils the just requirement of the law. Frequently this reference to the fulfilment of the just requirement of the law has been understood as a reference to our being justified by faith and being granted the righteousness of Christ. Paul, however, is not speaking here of the position of righteousness which has been granted to us by faith, that is, the forensic or legal standing which the Christian possesses before God. This is clear from verses 5–6, which speak about the believer's life or living in the Spirit rather than a righteous standing before God. Paul is referring in verse 4 to the fact that believers in Christ, while possessing a forensic standing, are also now walking by the Spirit and thus can truly love God with the whole heart, soul, and mind, and their neighbor as themselves. He is referring to the fact that believers now keep the law as the Old Testament meant it to be kept—in faith, in trust, and in constant dependence on the grace of God for forgiveness and cleansing. To use Pauline terminology, we can say that the believer lives by a faith working through love (Gal. 5:6), and in so doing keeps the law.

Although Paul saw the ceremonial law as no longer binding (Rom. 7:1–4) but as only a shadowy portrayal of what was to come in Christ (Col. 2:17), he could at times surrender his liberty in Christ and voluntarily place himself under the ceremonial demands of the Old Testament law in order not to hinder his witness to his Jewish kin (Rom. 14:13–23; see also Acts 21:19–26; 16:1–4). While Christians are not under the law in the sense of having to achieve or maintain their salvation legalistically, Paul claimed that Christians nevertheless keep the intent of the law, for they are able to love God and neighbor as God intended and thus fulfil the law (Rom. 13:8; Gal. 5:14).

It is, of course, true that the believer will many times fail and fall, for we are sinners not merely by choice but also by nature, and until the resurrection we will fall short of the glory of God time and time again. But the Lord has taught us to pray, "Forgive us our debts" (Matt. 6:12); and we have the promise of Scripture that "if we confess our sins, he [God] is faithful and just, and will forgive our sins and cleanse us from all unrighteousness" (1 John 1:9). So we delight in the law of God and meditate on it day and night (Ps. 1:2). We also keep the law, ever mindful that we do not do so in order to establish a relationship with God, for we are already justified and stand before him by faith alone. Rather, because the law is a reflection of the will of God for us, we seek to keep the law in order to be pleasing to our heavenly Father. Born again through God's Spirit, we can in our innermost being love God and neighbor and keep the law as God has commanded his sinful, fallen, but redeemed people. We do not keep the law perfectly, but we keep it in our new nature as we never could before and in constant dependence on the heavenly Father's grace and forgiveness. Understood in this manner, Paul's teaching on the law is not contradictory.

Every serious interpreter of the Scriptures has heard at some time or other a statement like, "Read it in its context," or "Keep in mind the context." This is good advice. Authors surround words and sentences with other words and sentences which they hope will provide clues in the interpretative process. It is foolish indeed not to make the most of these clues which an author provides to the reader. Time and time again difficulties and problems in interpretation are resolved when we pay careful attention to the context of the author. After all, what better commentary is there than that of the author, who surrounds a verse with clues that help reveal its meaning? Therefore we should read the words and their grammatical construction in their authorial context.

4

Understanding the Context

Other Biblical Books

In past generations the unity of the Bible was assumed as a given by the majority of Christians. This view was built on the belief that the Bible was uniquely inspired by God and thus could not contradict itself. At times the reverse was also argued: the unity of all its parts was one of the evidences of the inspiration of the Bible. Because of this presumed unity the Reformers developed a hermeneutical principle called the analogy of faith, which affirms that all biblical teachings are part of the revelation of God and thus any one part can and should be interpreted in light of the whole. This view is not as universally held as it once was, and some would minimize using the writings of one author of Scripture to cast light on the writings of another. It would appear, however, that completely apart from the matter of inspiration, one part of the Bible can prove quite useful in shedding light on another part. After all, the writers of the New Testament were well versed in the thoughts of the Old Testament; it was, in fact, their Bible! As a result, passages in the Old Testament may prove quite useful in interpreting parts of the New Testament dealing with similar themes. Furthermore, despite differences on various issues and in emphases, there was a great deal of commonality in the beliefs of the first-century Christian church. Whatever the differences, Christians certainly had more in common with one another than with other religions and philosophies. It seems only reasonable, therefore, to assume that there was a certain degree of common practices and beliefs, and that what one author reveals about a particular belief may help us to understand what another author, supposing his readers already knew it, did not explicitly mention. Our first example builds on the view that there was a great deal of agreement among the writers of the early church (and of course believers in general) concerning Christian baptism.

Is Baptism Necessary for Salvation?

One of the most common problems we encounter in the interpretation of the Bible is our tendency to understand the text in light of our own experience. This is especially true of passages which deal with doctrine and practice, or with the sacraments. A good example involves the numerous passages in the New Testament which speak of Christian baptism. Since most interpreters investigating these passages have experienced some form of baptism, it is not surprising that each has a tendency to interpret them, whether consciously or unconsciously, within the framework of his or her own experience.

In this section we will look at a number of New Testament passages on baptism which cause Baptists (as well as many pedobaptists) serious problems when they are understood in the light of the reader's personal experience of baptism. We shall then posit a thesis which will make sense of these passages by interpreting them in the light of what the first-century writers meant by them. Some of the most difficult passages are:

> And such [i.e., unrighteous] were some of you. But *you were washed,* you were sanctified, you were justified in the name of the Lord Jesus Christ and in the Spirit of our God. [1 Cor. 6:11, italics added]

> He saved us, not because of deeds done by us in righteousness, but in virtue of his own mercy, by *the washing of regeneration* and renewal in the Holy Spirit. [Titus 3:5, italics added]

> We were *buried therefore with him by baptism* into death, so that as Christ was raised from the dead by the glory of the Father, we too might walk in newness of life. [Rom. 6:4, italics added]

> *Baptism,* which corresponds to this, *now saves you,* not as a removal of dirt from the body but as an appeal to God for a clear conscience, through the resurrection of Jesus Christ. [1 Pet. 3:21, italics added]

Numerous attempts have been made to reconcile these passages with a traditional nonsacramentalist interpretation which claims that baptism has no immediate relationship to becoming a Christian, but comes either later, when one confesses saving faith by undergoing the rite, or earlier, when one is presented for baptism by one's parents. In this regard, it is usually denied that 1 Corinthians 6:11 and Titus 3:5 refer to baptism, and the term *washing* is seen as a metaphor which has nothing to do with Christian baptism. The burial with Christ in baptism of Romans 6:4 is seen as referring to a symbolic acting out in baptism either of what actually happened earlier when a person believed in Christ and was born again, or of a faith which is to come later. And 1 Peter 3:21 is sometimes interpreted as referring not to Christian baptism but to a "Spirit baptism."

While it is true that "washing" in 1 Corinthians 6:11 and Titus 3:5 is a metaphor, it does call to mind baptism, which involves the experience of being dipped into water. It should also be noted that in Titus 3:5 this experience of washing is intimately associated with renewal in the Holy Spirit, which calls to mind the tie between baptism and renewal in the Holy Spirit in the expression "the baptism of the Spirit." The Greek term translated "washing" (*loutron*), furthermore, was used by several non-Christian religions of that day to refer to baptism and was frequently used by the early church fathers to describe Christian baptism. In addition, the Greek verb translated "washed" in 1 Corinthians 6:11 is used only one other time in the New Testament: "And now why do you wait? Rise and be baptized, and wash away your sins, calling on his name" (Acts 22:16). Washing away one's sins is here clearly connected with baptism and with calling on Jesus' name. Calling on his name is likewise closely associated with baptism in Acts 2 (see vv. 21 and 38), and the related expression "in the name of Jesus Christ" appears to be a baptismal formula (Acts 10:48; see also 1 Cor. 1:13–15).

As for the reference to being buried with Christ through baptism, would it be legitimate to add to Romans 6:4 the parenthetical comment, "Of course we are not talking about baptism, but about the experience of conversion, which may occur years earlier or later and is symbolized by baptism"? There is not the slightest hint in this passage that Paul is referring to an experience which may occur weeks, months, or years before or after baptism. Nor is there any hint that the term *baptism* is to be interpreted symbolically. Finally, any attempt to fit 1 Peter 3:21 into our experience by explaining "baptism" here as some sort of "Spirit baptism" drowns in the flood waters mentioned in verse 20!

How, then, should we interpret these passages dealing with baptism as well as a passage like John 3:5, which refers to being "born of water and the Spirit"? Perhaps the simplest way of proceeding would be to formulate a thesis of how baptism and conversion are related, taking into consideration the teachings of the whole New Testament:

> In the New Testament, conversion, that is, becoming a Christian, involved five dimensions or aspects, all of which took place at the same time, that is, on the same day. These five dimensions were repentance, faith, confession, regeneration (or the receiving of the Holy Spirit), and baptism. To separate any of these in time does violence to the New Testament pattern.

Two major arguments can be advanced in support of this thesis: (1) the New Testament portrays various combinations of these dimensions in intimate association, and (2) each of these dimensions is said to bring about salvation.

We turn first to the various New Testament combinations of repentance, faith, confession, regeneration, and baptism:

1. At times faith and baptism are associated together. Paul says, "But now that faith has come, we are no longer under a custodian; for in Christ Jesus you are all sons of God, through faith. For as many of you were baptized into Christ have put on Christ" (Gal. 3:25–27). Note that Paul uses faith and baptism interchangeably in these verses. This is no problem if faith and baptism occurred at the same time, but if we separate them in time, the passage becomes difficult to interpret. Another example is Colossians 2:12: "And you were buried with him in baptism, in which you were also raised with him through faith in the working of God, who raised him from the dead." Here again baptism and faith are seen as occurring at the same time, for being buried (baptism) and being raised (faith) are a unity (see also Acts 16:31–33; 18:8).

2. At times faith and regeneration, that is, the reception of the Spirit, are associated together. In seeking to demonstrate to the Galatians that they were justified by faith alone, Paul asks, "Did you receive the Spirit by works of the law, or by hearing with faith?" (Gal. 3:2). The answer,

of course, is that they received the Spirit when they believed (see also Gal. 3:14; Eph. 1:13).

3. At times baptism and regeneration, that is, the receiving of the Spirit, are associated together. Titus 3:5 is an illustration. We might also mention the New Testament references to the baptism of the Spirit (Matt. 3:11; Mark 1:8; Luke 3:16; John 1:33; Acts 1:5; 11:16), each of which makes an explicit comparison between the baptism of John the Baptist and that of Jesus. John's baptism was one of repentance, whereas Jesus' was to be a baptism of the Spirit. We see no reason for the term *baptism* in this contrast to refer to two separate things. On the contrary, what we have here are the water baptism of John, which is associated with repentance, and Christian water baptism, which is associated with the coming of the Spirit. This lends support to the view that baptism and regeneration occurred on the same day.

In Romans 6:4, although the Spirit is not explicitly mentioned, baptism is associated with dying with Christ and walking in "newness of life." Since Romans 7:6, in the only other New Testament use of the term translated "newness" (*kainotēti*), speaks of "the new life of the Spirit," it seems reasonable to conclude that "newness of life," which is associated with baptism, and "the new life of the Spirit" are synonymous (see also the association of baptism and regeneration in Acts 9:17–18; 10:44–48).

4. At times faith and confession are associated. Here all we need to do is quote Paul's well-known words, "If you confess with your lips that Jesus is Lord and believe in your heart that God raised him from the dead, you will be saved" (Rom. 10:9).

5. At times baptism and confession are associated. In Acts 22:16 Ananias tells Paul, "And now why do you wait? Rise and be baptized, and wash away your sins, calling on his name."

6. At times faith and repentance are associated. At the beginning of Jesus' ministry he states, "The time is

fulfilled, and the kingdom of God is at hand; repent, and believe in the gospel'' (Mark 1:15). To this we can add Paul's words reminding the Ephesian elders that he did not shrink from preaching to them the entire counsel of God, ''testifying both to Jews and to Greeks of repentance to God and of faith in our Lord Jesus Christ'' (Acts 20:21).

7. At times repentance, baptism, and regeneration are associated. A good example is found in Acts 2:38. When Peter is asked by his audience as to what they should do, he replies, ''Repent, and be baptized every one of you in the name of Jesus Christ for the forgiveness of your sins; and you shall receive the gift of the Holy Spirit.'' Here repentance and baptism are associated with the gift of the Spirit, that is, regeneration, which comes when one repents and is baptized. Another example is found in Acts 11:15–18. When Peter recounted to the Jewish Christians in Jerusalem that he had baptized a Gentile named Cornelius because he had received the Spirit, ''they glorified God, saying, 'Then to the Gentiles also God has granted repentance unto life.'''

8. At times faith, baptism, regeneration, and repentance are associated. In Acts 19 Paul encounters some disciples in Ephesus, but notices that something is wrong. He then asks a simple yet clear question to determine whether they are Christians or not, ''Did you receive the Holy Spirit when you believed?'' (v. 2). When they answer in the negative by stating that they have not even heard of a Holy Spirit, Paul knows that they are not Christians. To his follow-up question, ''Into what then were you baptized?'' (v. 3), they reply that they were baptized into the baptism of John the Baptist. Paul responds, '''John baptized with the baptism of repentance, telling the people to believe in the one who was to come after him, that is, Jesus.' On hearing this, they were baptized in the name of the Lord Jesus. And when Paul had laid his hands upon them, the Holy Spirit came on them; and they spoke with tongues and prophesied'' (vv. 4–6). Here we should note that in

verse 4 Paul recognizes not only the need for repentance as preached by John, but also the need for faith in Jesus Christ. In verse 5 we read of the disciples' being baptized, and in verse 6 of their receiving the Spirit.

It would seem reasonable to conclude that all five of these dimensions (repentance, faith, confession, regeneration, and baptism) were understood as being involved in the experience of conversion. At times one or more of them may, according to the particular emphasis of the writer, be omitted from the account, but although omitted they are both assumed and implied. When Peter says, "Repent, and be baptized every one of you in the name of Jesus Christ for the forgiveness of your sins; and you shall receive the gift of the Holy Spirit" (Acts 2:38), he does not mention the need for faith. Yet certainly it must be assumed that faith is also required for his listeners' conversion. To deny this would mean that Peter is saying, "To receive the gift of the Holy Spirit you do not have to believe so long as you repent and are baptized." By any New Testament standard this is clearly absurd. Likewise, when Paul says, "If you confess with your lips that Jesus is Lord and believe in your heart that God raised him from the dead, you will be saved" (Rom. 10:9), he is not saying that we are saved by an act consisting exclusively of confession and faith. Regeneration, baptism, and repentance, although not mentioned, must be assumed. It seems clear, therefore, by the varied groupings of these dimensions throughout the New Testament that the experience of conversion was understood to involve all five of them and that they took place on the same day. As a result, when we read an account or come across a passage in which one or more of these aspects are missing, we ought to presume that although not mentioned, they are assumed by the speakers or writers.

We turn now to the argument that each of the five aspects is said to bring about salvation:

1. At times salvation is said to come about through

repentance. A good example of this is found in 2 Peter 3:9: "The Lord is not slow about his promise as some count slowness, but is forbearing toward you, not wishing that any should perish, but that all should reach repentance" (see also 2 Cor. 7:10; Luke 13:3; Acts 3:19; 11:18).

2. At times salvation is said to come about through faith. There are numerous examples of this, one of the most familiar being where Paul tells the Philippian jailor, "Believe in the Lord Jesus, and you will be saved" (Acts 16:31; see also Eph. 2:8–9).

3. At times salvation is said to come about through confession. After Paul declares that whoever confesses that Jesus is Lord and believes that God raised him from the dead will be saved (Rom. 10:9), we read, "For, 'every one who calls upon the name of the Lord will be saved'" (10:13).

4. At times salvation is said to come about through regeneration. Regardless of how we interpret Titus 3:5 with regard to the question of baptism, one thing is clear—salvation comes about "by the washing of regeneration." This is similar to Jesus' words in John 3:3, 5, where the expression "kingdom of God" is used as a synonym for "salvation." To enter the kingdom of God, that is, to acquire salvation, one must be born again of the Spirit.

5. At times salvation is said to come about through baptism. Here once again we can mention 1 Peter 3:21, where baptism is clearly said to save. The only way that we can separate baptism from salvation in this statement is by attributing to the word *baptism* a meaning different from what it usually bears.

Other blessings which are said to be brought about by baptism as well as by faith are forgiveness (cf. Acts 2:38 and 22:16 with Acts 10:43 and Rom. 4:3–8), union with Christ (cf. Gal. 3:27 with Eph. 3:17), and sonship with God (cf. Gal. 3:26–27 with John 1:12).

From all that has been said it would appear that our thesis has been demonstrated: In the New Testament, conversion involved five dimensions or aspects, all of which took place at the same time, that is, on the same day. These five dimensions were repentance, faith, confession, regeneration (or the receiving of the Holy Spirit), and baptism. To separate any of these in time does violence to the New Testament pattern, which involved three parties: the individual, who repented of sin, believed in Christ, and confessed Jesus as Lord; God, who gave his Spirit and brought about the individual's rebirth; and the church, which baptized the individual.

At this point we must note that although baptism was part of the process and necessary for becoming a Christian in New Testament times, it did not automatically bring about regeneration. Paul in 1 Corinthians 1:13–17 and 10:1–6 indicates rather clearly that baptism does not magically bring about a person's salvation or regeneration. Individuals were born again or saved because upon repenting, believing, and confessing their faith, God graciously forgave them and through the gift of his Spirit made them a new creation. Baptism was the visible sign which God ordained as the initiation rite for entrance into the Christian faith. Hypothetically, it is true that one could enter the kingdom of God apart from baptism (the thief on the cross is a pointed example). But the normal manner by which one became a Christian involved being baptized on the same day. To refuse to be baptized was unheard of, and such a refusal would have exposed an unwillingness to repent and submit to what God had ordained. (That it was the refusal to submit to baptism rather than the lack of baptism which would damn is clearly the view of the postbiblical addition found in Mark 16:16, which reads, "He who believes and is baptized will be saved; but he who does not believe will be condemned.")

Perhaps an illustration will help. If in our culture the act of placing a gold ring on the third finger of the left hand were reserved exclusively to the marriage ceremony, and everyone who married did so, it is quite easy to see how a gold ring on the third finger of the left hand would become intimately associated with getting married. The question, "When were you married?" could even be reworded to, "When did you put the ring on your finger?" In fact, getting married could easily be referred to as "putting on the ring," even though other things such as obtaining the marriage license, the repeating of certain vows, and the sexual consummation, would also be involved in the process. In like manner, baptism in the New Testament is so intimately connected with becoming a Christian that becoming a Christian (getting married) can be referred to as being baptized (putting on a wedding ring). But, and this is no small but, it is always assumed that baptism is accompanied by repentance, faith, confession, and regeneration (a wedding license, vows, the sexual consummation).

Problems would, of course, develop if certain people began to place gold wedding rings on the third finger of their left hands in anticipation of a future marriage (i.e., before the wedding) or perhaps on their fifth anniversary (i.e., after the wedding). The original meaning of the gold wedding ring would be shattered, and its intimate connection with getting married would be destroyed. "When did you put the ring on your finger?" would no longer be synonymous with "When were you married?" Furthermore, comments made when gold wedding rings were put on only at the time of marriage would now tend to be misunderstood, for the later situation and practice conflict with the earlier.

In a similar way the present-day practices of baptizing people long before faith (pedobaptism) or after faith (believer's baptism) make it difficult to understand the new Testament teaching on the subject in that we tend to interpret these passages in light of our own experience. In the Book of Acts, however, baptism is intimately connected with conversion. With few (if any) exceptions it occurred on the same day. The Philippian jailor was baptized the very night of his conversion (Acts 16:33); the Ethiopian eunuch was baptized immediately (Acts 8:36–38). Baptism for them was less a testimony and confession to the world than part of the process of becoming a Christian.

The basic purpose of our discussion has not been to recommend how baptism should be practiced today. This is properly the task of a systematic theologian. Rather, the basic purpose has been to offer help in interpreting the New Testament passages dealing with baptism. Instead of interpreting them in terms of our own experience and trying to make their meaning conform to it, we need to understand how the New Testament writers viewed the relationship between baptism and conversion and what they meant to say in those passages we find difficult. By looking at the entire biblical context on this subject we are able to acquire an overall conception of baptism and make sense of many troublesome individual passages.

What Does It Mean That Paul Speaks and "Not the Lord"? (1 Cor. 7:10, 12)

In 1 Corinthians 7:10 and 12 we find two statements which have caused interpreters serious difficulties in that it appears as if the apostle Paul is denying that what he says comes from God. In verse 12 he states:

> To the rest I say, not the Lord, that if any brother has a wife who is an unbeliever, and she consents to live with him, he should not divorce her.

The problem this verse creates is heightened by the fact that in verse 10 Paul has just said:

> To the married I give charge, not I but the Lord, that the wife should not separate from her husband.

It appears, at first glance at least, that Paul in verse 10 is claiming divine authority for what he is saying in that it comes from the Lord, whereas in verse 12 what he is saying is not from the Lord at all, but simply his own view.

Is Paul in 1 Corinthians 7:12 claiming that what he says stands in opposition to what God has proclaimed to be his will? Or is Paul saying that he knows that what he has said in verse 10 comes from God, but that he is unsure of whether what he says in verse 12 is the will of God? In either instance we have a problem, for how can we accept verses 12–16 as the Word of God if they conflict with what God says elsewhere or if Paul is simply expressing his own uninspired opinion?

This problem is more apparent than real, however, for when we understand what Paul means in verse 10 the problem disappears. There is a parallel to verse 10 in 1 Corinthians 9:14, where Paul states, "In the same way, the Lord commanded that those who proclaim the gospel should get their living by the gospel." For each of these verses there is also a parallel in the Synoptic Gospels. Luke 10:7, the parallel to 1 Corinthians 9:14, reads, "For the laborer [the preacher of the gospel] deserves his wages"; Mark 10:11–12, the parallel to 1 Corinthians 7:10, reads, "Whoever divorces his wife and marries another, commits adultery against her; and if she divorces her husband and marries another, she commits adultery" (see also Luke 16:18). Note that the words of the Lord which Paul gives in 1 Corinthians 7:10 and 9:14 closely resemble words spoken by the Lord Jesus during his ministry (see also 1 Cor. 11:23–26 and Mark 14:22–24).

What Paul means in 1 Corinthians 7:10 is that the statement concerning divorce which he is about to make comes from Jesus' teachings. Although Paul is writing ("to the married I give charge"), ultimately his teaching comes from Jesus ("not I but the Lord"). Jesus had taught that wives should not divorce their husbands and vice versa, and Paul is quoting this dominical tradition here. However, Jesus in his ministry never dealt with the issue of mixed marriages in which one partner is a believer and the other is not, so Paul states that on this issue he has no word from the teachings of Jesus that is applicable (1 Cor. 7:12).

As a result he now gives his own apostolic teaching. (Cf. 1 Cor. 7:25, where Paul states, "Now concerning the unmarried, I have no command of the Lord, but I give my opinion as one who by the Lord's mercy is trustworthy.") That Paul does not doubt his divine authority in what he says in 1 Corinthians 7:12–16 is evident from verse 40: "And I think that I have the Spirit of God."

A second problem that is raised by 1 Corinthians 7:12–16 is the apparent conflict we find here with Jesus' teachings on this subject as recorded in Mark 10:11 and Luke 16:18. The Markan and Lukan accounts give no grounds whatsoever for divorce. Paul, however, seems to permit divorce in the case of desertion by the non-Christian partner (1 Cor. 7:15). Moreover, in Matthew 5:32 and 19:9 we have the famous exception clause which permits divorce in the case of adultery. The problem can be worded simply as follows: "Did Jesus forbid divorce absolutely as it appears in Mark 10:11 and Luke 16:18, or did he permit divorce in the case of adultery as we find in Matthew 5:32 and 19:9, and in the case of desertion by the unbelieving partner as we find in 1 Corinthians 7:15?"

This question has been debated for centuries, and all the arguments and views cannot be presented here. Instead, we will suggest a solution which we hope will do justice to all the evidence. It appears that what is found in Mark and Luke is closer to the actual words of Jesus than are the Matthean accounts. One evidence of this is that the Markan and Lukan forms are more difficult: it is easier to see why Matthew would add an interpretive comment (the exception clause) than why Mark and Luke (and Paul in quoting Jesus in 1 Cor. 7:10) would have made the saying more difficult. Second, we have three independent witnesses (Mark, Luke, Paul) who record a form of Jesus' saying which does not have the exception clause; only Matthew includes this clause.

Assuming that Jesus did not give any exception in his prohibition of divorce, how are we to explain what Matthew has done in 5:32 and 19:9, and Paul in 1 Corinthians 7:15? One feature of Jesus' teachings that we frequently encounter is his use of hyperbolic language. For example:

> If any one comes to me and does not hate his own father and mother and wife and children and brothers and sisters, yes, and even his own life, he cannot be my disciple. [Luke 14:26]
>
> You blind guides, straining out a gnat and swallowing a camel! [Matt. 23:24]
>
> It is easier for a camel to go through the eye of a needle than for a rich man to enter the kingdom of God. [Mark 10:25]
>
> If your right eye causes you to sin, pluck it out and throw it away; it is better that you lose one of your members than that your whole body be thrown into hell. [Matt. 5:29]

We could cite many other examples, but it is sufficiently clear that Jesus did use hyperbolic language in his teachings. No doubt he did so for mnemonic purposes, that is, to help his hearers remember his teachings, for the use of hyperbole creates a deep impression and is easily remembered. Another reason Jesus used such language was to reveal the intensity which he felt for the subject. This is certainly true with regard to the matter of divorce.

In the context of Mark 10 Jesus is asked to enter into the rabbinic debate concerning the legitimate causes for a man to divorce his wife (Mark 10:2). In the debate over what constituted an "indecency" and thus legitimized divorce according to Deuteronomy 24:1–4, various positions were taken. Rabbi Shammai and his followers took a more conservative stance and argued that only unchastity on the part of the wife was a legitimate reason. Rabbi Hillel and his followers, however, took a much more liberal approach and argued that divorce was legitimate if a wife burned the evening meal or if the husband found someone more attractive. When Jesus was asked what constituted a legitimate ground for divorce, he protested strongly against this whole attitude and pointed out that divorce was contrary to the divine pattern and goal, and that God had from the very beginning intended a lifelong monogamous relationship between a man and a woman (Mark 10:3–9). In affirming the divine pattern for marriage—that marriage was to be "until death us do part"—Jesus had no intention of giving a hypothetical situation in which divorce was permissible, for if he did (we are assuming for the sake of argument that he knew of one or two), the focus of attention would fall on the possible exceptions rather than on the divine plan and pattern, which was that marriage should not be "put asunder" (v. 9). As a result, he used an overstatement to express his view.

How do we know that Jesus was using a hyperbole in this instance? By noting that Matthew in the two instances where he presents the same material found in Mark 10:11 and Luke 16:18 adds his exception clause. This indicates that in Matthew's understanding Jesus was not laying down an absolute law which would cover all circumstances. With divine authority the Evangelist interprets Jesus' words as a forbidding of divorce but not in an absolute sense. Having the mind of Christ, he is aware that the horror of adultery does pose a legitimate ground for divorce. Even as surgery is never a good thing but may be the lesser of two evils, at times divorce is less evil than a union in which adultery has taken place.

That the apostle Paul was also familiar with Jesus' basic teaching on divorce is evident from 1 Corinthians 7:10. Yet Paul, too, was aware of a situation when divorce is permissible, namely, when "the unbelieving partner desires to separate" (1 Cor. 7:15). Such an action was never to be initiated by the Christian (note vv. 12–14), but if the unbelieving partner "desires to separate [divorce]," then the Christian "is not bound." ("Not bound" almost certainly means "free to remarry," since separation in the sense of simply no longer sharing bed and board is a later idea.) So Paul, possessing the Spirit of God (1 Cor. 7:40), interprets Jesus' teaching as not excluding divorce in the case of desertion.

Does Paul's teaching in 1 Corinthians 7:15 conflict with Jesus' teachings? The answer is no! He, like Matthew, knew well Jesus' teaching on the subject and interpreted it as a strong prohibition of easy divorce and a strong affirmation of the divine pattern given at creation. For both Paul and Matthew divorce is an evil. There is no such thing as a good divorce. The divine pattern is for marriage to last until death parts the one-flesh union. Jesus' abhorrence of divorce is clearly revealed by the way in which he condemned it. One tends to use exaggerated language when one feels strongly about a subject, for such language tends to impress and persuade. The few exceptions where divorce is the lesser of two evils Jesus did not wish to elucidate. Both Matthew and Paul, however, faced specific issues in their church communities which needed to be resolved. In dealing with these specific instances (adultery, and desertion by an unbelieving partner) they follow Jesus in affirming the divine pattern of marriage, but they also acknowledge two situations in which divorce is permissible as the lesser of two evils. In so doing they possess apostolic authority and the mind of Christ.

What Is the Standard for Orthodoxy? (1 John 4:2–3)

The New Testament contains a number of letters which were occasioned by a major theological problem. The book which most obviously fits into this category is Paul's letter to the Galatians; another is 1 Corinthians. Yet another letter which emerged out of a major theological controversy is 1 John. It is somewhat unclear as to exactly what the problem was, but Irenaeus writing around A.D. 180 states that it centered around a Gnostic named Cerinthus, who taught that Jesus was not born of a virgin but was the natural son of Joseph and Mary, and that the Christ descended upon him after his baptism and withdrew from him just before his suffering and death. Associated with this view was a dualistic philosophy which viewed matter (and thus the body) negatively. The incarnation was denied in order to save the divine Christ from being contaminated with a body. That this error involved both ethics (1 John 1:6, 8, 10; 2:4) and Christology (1 John 1:1–4; 4:1–6; 5:6; cf. 2 John 7) is evident.

How did John deal with this christological issue? In 1 John 4:1 he writes, "Beloved, do not believe every spirit, but test the spirits to see whether they are of God; for many false prophets have gone out into the world." John tells his readers that they should stop believing (the imperative is in the present tense, which implies that his readers should cease doing something they are presently doing) every spirit, that is, every utterance or person supposedly inspired by the Spirit. On the contrary such spirits are to be continually tested (again a present imperative). The reason for this is evident. There are both true and false prophets. If one does not test their interpretations, one will not be able to distinguish between the true and the false, between the divine and the satanic. A childlike trust in the divine promises is praiseworthy, but a childlike faith in the demonic is not. Before we make a leap of faith we must be sure that we are leaping into the hands of God rather than Satan.

John therefore tells his readers that they should test the various views that they are hearing concerning the Savior. No doubt the reason for this was that a false view about him was circulating among the churches, a position that had its roots not in divine revelation but in the "spirit of antichrist" (1 John 4:3). Yet how were John's readers to make such a test? How were they to distinguish truth from falsehood, orthodoxy from heresy? Speaking from what he himself has witnessed (1 John 1:1–4) and using his apostolic authority, John gives a test. Even as the color of a piece of litmus paper reveals immediately if a solution is an acid or a base, so the apostle provides a test by which his readers will immediately be able to tell if a christological view is true or false: "By this [test] you know the Spirit of God: every spirit which confesses that Jesus Christ has come in the flesh is of God, and every spirit which does not confess Jesus is not of God" (4:2–3a).

Although the exact nature of the christological problem is unclear, it is evident from the test given by John that it involved the denial of the humanity of the Son of God and his oneness with Jesus. This is confirmed by 2 John 7, where the apostle states, "For many deceivers have gone out into the world, men who will not acknowledge the coming of Jesus Christ in the flesh." The christological heresy John was combating denied that the Son of God truly became a man. It may have even separated the human Jesus from the Christ, claiming that the Christ descended on Jesus later and was never identical with him. Here then was the test for orthodoxy. Here was the litmus paper which could be used to determine truth from error. A person who confessed belief that Jesus Christ, the Son of God, came in the flesh, was of the truth. And whoever denied the true humanity of Jesus Christ, the Son of God, that is, whoever denied that Jesus took on himself real flesh, was heretical and of the evil one.

In 1 John 5:6 John adds that Jesus, the Son of God, "came by water and blood . . . not with the water only but with the water and the blood." The twofold reference to water and blood is probably best interpreted not as a reference to Jesus' baptism and the Lord's Supper, nor to the incarnation in general, nor to Jesus' baptism and death, but to the death of the Son of God. The closest parallel to this is found in John 19:34 (which was either written by the author of 1 John or well known by him): at the death of Jesus "blood and water" flowed from his side. This would fit well the statement of Irenaeus that one of the problems facing John was the view that the Christ-spirit descended on the human Jesus only after his baptism and departed before his death. No, says John, Jesus Christ, the Son of God, came in water and blood. The Jesus Christ who has come in the flesh truly died!

The test for orthodoxy, then, was the confession "Jesus Christ has come in the flesh." But is this really *the only* test for orthodoxy? It is important at this point to distinguish between the original meaning of our text and its present-day significance. John clearly meant that this belief was to be *the* test for orthodoxy *for his readers*. In the context in which John wrote his letter the litmus test for orthodoxy was clearly the confession that Jesus Christ had come in the flesh. This was not simply a test of a better theology. It was the test of true or false religion, of a divine revelation or a human philosophy. To deny the humanity of Jesus Christ was heretical and still is. But while the incarnation is a test for orthodoxy, is it still *the only* test for orthodoxy?

Whereas the particular issue confronting the readers of 1 John involved denial of the humanity of Jesus Christ, so that confession of the humanity of the Son of God could be *the* test for orthodoxy, today this is not the primary issue facing the church. Relatively few people today would deny the true humanity of the one whom the Bible calls Jesus of Nazareth. Both believers and unbelievers are willing to accept the true humanity of Jesus. (We shall leave aside the question of whether some theologians of our day are essentially Docetic and deny in principle the humanity of Jesus Christ.) Since even unbelievers are willing to acknowledge the humanity of Jesus Christ, this clearly cannot be *the* test for orthodoxy today.

The situation today is different from that faced by 1 John, for the kinds of errors which the modern church faces are different. And even more significant is the fact that we do not have an apostle like John to formulate a test to cover today's problems. On the other hand, while we may lack an apostolic authority, we do possess a canonical authority. We have in the Scriptures the only infallible rule for faith and practice. The variety of revelation in the Bible and the fact that it is not a catechism nor a systematized collection of theological beliefs remind us, however, that if we should attempt to establish canonical tests for orthodoxy, we must do so only with great care and reverence—with care lest we read into the Scriptures our own personal biases, and with reverence lest we make God a liar! With such caveats ever in view, it may at times be helpful, in light of certain false teachings, to establish out of the teachings of Scripture a litmus test which will enable the church to judge truth from error.

In the past such tests have served the church well. In the christological debates of the early church, *homoousios* (Jesus is the same as the Father in essence) and *homoiousios* (Jesus is like the Father in essence) separated orthodoxy and Arianism. "Justification by faith alone" was the central test during the Reformation. At the turn of the twentieth century some evangelical Christians formulated a platform of five "fundamentals" which were to distinguish evangelical from liberal Christianity. These five were the inerrancy of the Scriptures, the deity of Jesus Christ, the virgin birth, the substitutionary atonement, and the bodily resurrection and imminent physical return of the Lord. Such tests while helpful should not be considered as the sum total of the Christian faith. They were useful and helpful at the time, but are not to be isolated from the rest of the teachings of Scripture, for their effectiveness may become dated with the rise of other issues in the church.

It is necessary for the church to test the spirits continually (1 John 4:1). Christians are not to believe every message or interpretation that they hear. Furthermore, truth is not dependent on which preacher or teacher is proclaiming the message or interpretation, for fame and reputation are not tests of the truth. The evangelical claim has always been that the Bible is the only infallible rule of faith and practice. No true spirit will conflict with the Scriptures; all true teachers will welcome any use of the Word of God to test their messages. Even historical creeds and confessions are not infallible but are true only to the degree that they agree with the Scriptures.

The church needs both to test the spirits (1 John 4:1) and to be nonjudgmental (Matt. 7:1–5). Each of these practices can become dangerous in isolation from the other. Many a local church and denomination have suffered from overzealous guardians of orthodoxy who are continually seeking out error and finding heresy lurking behind every bush. Eventually this mentality becomes so divisive that only two individuals remain, and each of these is not too certain about the other! On the other hand, there is also a danger of being oblivious to the Scriptures' warnings of fierce wolves (Acts 20:29–30), false prophets (Matt. 7:15), and false Christs (Mark 13:22) who will come and not spare the flock. These two concerns of the church must be held in tension; regard for truth should arise out of a love for God and for his people.

Once Saved, Always Saved? (Heb. 6:4–6)

Within the New Testament there are a number of passages which believers throughout the history of the church have found comforting and reassuring. These give assurance to Christians that they need not worry about the future, for as God's people they have nothing to fear. We are God's children, and as his children we can be confident "that he who began a good work in [us] will bring it to completion at the day of Jesus Christ" (Phil. 1:6). As Christians we know that God is for us and that Christ shall be our advocate in the day of judgment (Rom. 8:31, 34).

> Who shall separate us from the love of Christ? Shall tribulation, or distress, or persecution, or famine, or nakedness, or peril, or sword? . . . No, in all these things we are more than conquerors through him who loved us. For I am sure that neither death, nor life, nor angels, nor principalities, nor things present, nor things to come, nor powers, nor

> height, nor depth, nor anything else in all creation, will be able to separate us from the love of God in Christ Jesus our Lord. [Rom. 8:35–39]

These are precious words indeed, and on the basis of these and similar passages and considerations some have argued that Christians are eternally secure, that is, that once they have been saved they can never lose that salvation. On the other hand, there are also passages in the New Testament which appear to warn believers lest they become apostate and lose their place among the people of God. A most important passage in this respect is found in Hebrews 6:4–6:

> For it is impossible to restore again to repentance those who have once been enlightened, who have tasted the heavenly gift, and have become partakers of the Holy Spirit, and have tasted the goodness of the word of God and the powers of the age to come, if they then commit apostasy, since they crucify the Son of God on their own account and hold him up to contempt.

As might be suspected, this passage is interpreted quite differently by those who hold to a doctrine of eternal security and by those who deny it. Frequently such views are described as Calvinism and Arminianism respectively, although both of these theological systems involve far more than just this one issue. As might be imagined, an Arminian interpretation tends to see in these verses a rather straightforward teaching that Christians who have at one time truly repented of their sins and been born again into the family of God (and thus "have become partakers of the Holy Spirit") can become apostate and lose the salvation they once possessed.

On the other hand, a Calvinist usually interprets this passage in one of two ways. One way is to claim that the persons spoken of in these verses were never true Christians. Whereas they had become involved in the Christian community, had been illuminated by the Holy Spirit so that they both knew and were convinced of the truth of the gospel message, and had even witnessed God's power and might, they had never truly become Christians. They had never been born again. As a result they could not have lost salvation in that they never possessed salvation. This is the way that John Calvin interpreted this passage. The second way in which this passage has been interpreted, although Calvin rejected this explanation, is to lay great weight on the "if" in verse 6. (Although the "if" is not in the Greek, the participle rendered "commit apostasy" [*parapesontas*] can be translated conditionally.) This interpretation argues that the passage refers to a purely hypothetical situation which in reality could never take place. The main problem with this interpretation is that the situation envisioned in this passage is clearly real and not simply imaginary.

The warning in these verses does not stand alone in the Book of Hebrews. We find similar warnings in 3:12–19; 10:26–31; and 12:25–29. The fact that the author often repeats this warning clearly reveals that we are not dealing simply with an imaginary, hypothetical situation. The author tells us six things about the people described in 6:4–6: (1) They professed *repentance*. Note that in verse 1 of this chapter repentance from dead works is associated with faith toward God. (2) They had been *enlightened*. This term is used once more in 10:32, where it refers to those who, in contrast to those who shrink back and are destroyed, "have faith and keep their souls" (10:39). (3) They have *tasted the heavenly gift*. Although some have suggested that this refers to participation in the Lord's Supper (as enlightenment allegedly refers to baptism), probably the best interpretation is to see the expression as a general metaphor for tasting the kindness (1 Pet. 2:3) and goodness (Ps. 34:8) of God. (4) They have *become partakers of the Holy Spirit*. The Greek term translated "partakers" is also used in 3:1 ("who share") for the readers who are further defined as "holy brethren," and in 3:14 ("we share"), where we find a similar warning. (5) They have *tasted the goodness of the Word of God*. Probably this can best be interpreted to mean that they have tasted the good Word of God. (6) Finally, they are described as *having tasted the powers of the age to come*. This apparently refers to the signs, wonders, and miracles which accompanied the preaching of the gospel message they heard (2:4).

It is evident that when we interpret a passage of Scripture, we do so in light of the overall understanding which we bring to the text. Whether this is good or bad is irrelevant. It is simply a fact. We interpret any portion of Scripture by means of our existing understanding of the Scripture as a whole. At the same time, however, our understanding of the particular part of Scripture is helping shape our understanding of the Scripture as a whole. Here we encounter once again the phenomenon of interpretation referred to as the hermeneutical circle. We cannot interpret any passage of Scripture without at the same time having our general understanding of Scripture (our theological system) play a major role. On the other hand, our interpretation of any particular passage is also helping shape our general understanding of the teachings of Scripture. Since our theological understanding is not infallible, since we know only in part, our system must always be open to change. At times we may come across a passage that does not seem to fit our system. A single such passage is seldom sufficient to refute it, but if we come across other passages which appear to contradict our system, we shall have to make certain modifications and changes to fit the new evidence.

In actuality the doctrine of eternal security is usually less dependent on individual passages of Scripture than on the overall theological system which one brings to these passages. This is not always recognized, but it is nevertheless true. (It may be less true, however, for lay people than it is for theologians.) In this regard I remember a television evangelist who in the same sermon vigorously condemned (actually damned as originating in hell) the theological system called Calvinism and those who deny the doctrine of eternal security. The irony in all this is that the doctrine of eternal security stems for the most part from a Calvinistic theological system. It was due to Calvin's belief in the doctrine of predestination and unconditional election that he came to believe in the doctrine of eternal security. And the fact is that he was far less convinced of the latter than the former! Calvin realized that if the doctrine of eternal security was to be based on something more than mere wishing on our part, it required the system of theology which we call Calvinism. The only sure basis for the eternal security of the Christian is the sovereign predestination of God. (For those familiar with the five cardinal points of Calvinism this means that eternal security, i.e., the perseverance of the saints, is dependent and based on the doctrines of total depravity, unconditional election, limited atonement, and irresistible grace.)

At this point it may be helpful to define such expressions as "eternal security" and "once saved, always saved." These are not the best ways to describe this theological concept. A far better expression is the "perseverance of the saints." Here the thought is that the believer will persevere in faith until the end. This is a much more biblical way of expressing the concept. If it is understood in this manner, there is little practical difference between a Calvinistic and an Arminian view on this subject. Calvinism argues that by God's grace true believers will continue in faith until they meet the Lord. From this it is concluded that someone who does not persevere in faith never had true faith, that is, never truly was a Christian. First John 2:19—"They went out from us, but they were not of us; for if they had been of us, they would have continued with us; but they went out, that it might be plain that they all are not of us"—is often used as an illustration. A person who does not persevere is lost and in fact was never saved.

On the other hand, the Arminian position also states that Christians must by God's grace persevere in the faith. If they do not persevere, they have become apostate, have rejected the faith, and are now lost. Whereas once they were saved, now they are lost. Note that the result is the same for both the Arminian and the Calvinist: whoever does not persevere in the faith is lost! Whether the individual once had saving faith and lost it (Arminianism), or never had saving faith to start with (Calvinism), both systems ultimately agree that the lack of a persevering faith means that the individual is lost in sin. Both agree that "he who is of God hears the words of God" (John 8:47), and that "by this we may be sure that we know him, if we keep his commandments" (1 John 2:3).

With regard to Hebrews 6:4–6 it is clear that any one of the six characteristics found in these verses can be interpreted as referring to someone who is not a true Christian, but when all six are grouped together, such an interpretation becomes much more difficult, if not impossible. As one who has always believed in the doctrine of eternal security, I must confess that this passage does indeed conflict with such a view. I have much less of a problem, however, with the more biblical concept of the perseverance of the saints. Yet in discussing this passage we must not lose sight of what the writer is saying. He is urging his readers to pay closer attention to the gospel message lest neglecting so great a salvation they receive a just retribution (Heb. 2:1–3), to take care lest there be within them an unbelieving heart leading them away from the living God (Heb. 3:12), to avoid the fearful prospect of judgment (Heb. 10:26), and to confirm their call and election (see 2 Pet. 1:10). Whether we are Calvinists or Arminians, the writer of Hebrews would urge us to pray with Bernard of Clairvaux, "Lord, let me never, never outlive my love to Thee."

We should interpret every passage of Scripture in its

context. This is especially true in cases where the passage seems to conflict with teachings found elsewhere in the Bible. The contexts to be kept in view as we interpret a passage include (in order of importance):

the immediate sentence in which the words are found

the paragraph in which the sentence is found

the chapter in which the paragraph is found

the letter in which the chapter is found

other writings of the same author

the New Testament

the Old Testament

The last two contexts have often been abused in the past; it is not uncommon for people to try to interpret a verse in Romans primarily through a verse in Revelation or in Genesis instead of through the verses which immediately precede and follow. This is, of course, a mistake, for the writers of Genesis and Revelation cannot contribute clues to the meaning of this verse to the degree that the author himself can by the immediate context. The chapter and the book in which the verse appear are likewise more valuable than the Psalms or Isaiah.

Nevertheless, we should not lose sight of the fact that at times an author, because of the very nature of his letter, may not provide clues which are important for understanding his meaning. He may not have had to provide such clues for his first-century readers, for he was able to build on a common knowledge and understanding which often came through personal acquaintance with the author. Unfortunately, today's readers lack that common knowledge and understanding, and so at times, as we have illustrated in this chapter, it is helpful to interpret a passage in light of the New Testament context. This is true even if all the members of the first-century church did not believe exactly alike. Whatever the diversity may have been in the early Christian community, there was, nevertheless, a greater unity of thought and values among believers than among the world at large. Knowing something of that unity, and for that matter also the diversity, provides us clues in understanding the meaning of an author. These clues are never as good as the clues that the author himself may give, but they are helpful.

We should also remember that the Old Testament was the Bible of the early church. Here, too, there was no doubt diversity in understanding and interpretation, but there was also a common world which was shared as the early church read and searched the Law, the Prophets, and the Writings. Someone like Paul would have been especially well versed in the Old Testament. Thus it is far more helpful to look for clues in the Old Testament than in such places as the mystery religions, various pagan cults, and later Gnosticism.

Some other contexts that may prove useful include the Jewish literature of the intertestamental period, the writings of the earliest church fathers, and contemporary Greek authors. These, however, are seldom as useful as the biblical materials themselves. We will not go wrong if we follow the Reformation principle of the analogy of faith: each Scripture is to be interpreted in light of the rest of Scripture.

5

Understanding Two Difficult Passages

A Comprehensive Approach

In the previous chapters we have discussed how to go about seeking to understand some of the difficult passages in the Epistles of the New Testament. The basic principles we set down are fundamental principles of biblical interpretation. More often than not, difficult passages can be resolved when we interpret them properly and discover what the authors meant by their words. We pointed out that a correct interpretation requires a correct understanding of the basic building blocks of literature—the words. First, we must obtain a correct understanding of the key words that an author uses in his writing. Second, we must then seek a correct understanding of how the author relates these words to one another. For this we need to know the syntax or grammatical relationships in which the author places these words. Neither of these steps can be isolated from the other, for there is a circular process in which the meaning of the sentence informs us as to the meaning of the individual words, and at the same time the meaning of the individual words informs us as to the meaning of the sentence.

In the third chapter we examined the importance of the authorial context. The circular process involved in interpretation continues beyond the sentence, for the meanings of the paragraph, the chapter, the book, and the other writings of the author provide us with clues to the meaning of the sentence, which is at the same time informing us of the meaning not only of the words, but also of the paragraph, chapter, book, and other writings. This hermeneutical process sounds much more complicated than it really is, for the mind is able to do all this simultaneously. It is, nevertheless, important for the interpreter to understand the logical procedure which is being followed. In chapter 4 we pointed out that at times the clues provided by the authorial context may be insufficient and that the larger context of the whole Bible may provide assistance as to the meaning of a text.

In this chapter we will look at two additional passages. The first will serve as an example of all the principles discussed in the preceding chapters; the second will raise the issue of difficult passages which may, at least for the present, elude resolution.

What Is the Sin unto Death? (1 John 5:16)

Within all of Scripture there is probably no single passage which causes more individual problems of interpretation than does 1 John 5:16. Whereas usually one particular problem in this passage receives the most attention, there exist numerous other difficulties as well. The passage reads:

> If any one sees his brother committing what is not a mortal sin, he will ask, and God will give him life for those whose sin is not mortal. There is sin which is mortal; I do not say that one is to pray for that.

In this verse various exegetical problems are encountered, the first two of which have to do with the understanding of key words:

1. Is there any difference in meaning between the words "ask" (*aitein*) and "pray" (*erōtan*)? Probably not. It seems best to see in the use of these two different but related terms a favorite Johannine stylistic device. John is fond of using synonyms. A good example of this is found in John 21:15–17, where John uses interchangeably two different words for "love" (*agapan* and *philein*) and the words *sheep* and *lambs*.

2. Another problem we encounter in our text involves the meaning of "mortal" (lit., "unto death"). Is this a reference to physical death as a result of sin? Here we might think of the example of Ananias and Sapphira (Acts 5:1–11) or of those who abused the communion table (1 Cor. 11:30). And when Jesus says, "This illness is not unto death" (John 11:4), he is referring to physical death. But since the nearest antecedent of the "life" which is prayed for in 1 John 5:16 is spiritual or eternal life (5:11–13), it would appear best to see the death being referred to here as spiritual death.

3. A third problem arises in the area of syntax (grammar): Who is it that gives life to the brother who has committed what is not a mortal sin? Is it the person who prayed for the sinner or is it God? While the Revised Standard Version reads, "God will give . . . life," there is a note in the margin which points out that the Greek text actually says "he." In favor of the view that "he" refers to the person who prayed is the fact that God is not mentioned. The verb *will give* is preceded by the verbs *sees* and *will ask*, and the subject of both these verbs is the believer who is praying for his brother. The subject of the next similar verb ("pray") is once again the believer. Grammatically, therefore, it makes good sense not to see any change in the subject of these verbs, for John does not indicate that there is such a change.

On the other hand, a point in favor of seeing "God" as the subject of "will give" is the theological fact that no human being can give eternal life to another human being. This is something God alone can do. Probably the best way of resolving this question is to recognize that the ultimate source of eternal life is God, but that the believer by prayer may act as a mediate cause in the sinner's receiving of life. Even though God alone brings healing to the sick, yet the prayers of faithful believers serve as the instrumental means of this healing (James 5:14–15). The believer can serve in a parallel capacity in regard to those who have committed a nonmortal sin.

4. A fourth problem that arises can be resolved by investigating the authorial context. Whose soul is saved by the believer's asking? Who is the "him" to whom God will give life? Is it the one praying or the sinner being prayed for? Actually the grammar permits either possibility, but the general flow of the argument indicates that it is the sinner who is granted life. This finds support in verses 14–15, which speak of God's hearing and granting believers' requests; and in this particular case, of course, the request involves the situation of the sinner. (See also James 5:15, where prayer saves the sick man from death.)

Other problems raised by 1 John 5:16 can be solved by looking to the biblical canon:

5. Whereas the person described as committing a nonmortal sin is clearly referred to as a "brother," that is, a Christian, what kind of a person is it who commits the sin unto death? Is this individual likewise a brother or a non-Christian? Our text does not say. The decision we make on this question will be determined by our theological position concerning the perseverance of the saints, that is, eternal security.

6. Is the writer expressly forbidding Christians to pray for those who have committed the sin unto death, or is he simply refraining from urging them to do so? In rare instances in Scripture we find God forbidding believers to

pray for someone or something. Jeremiah is told by the Lord, "Do not pray for the welfare of this people" (Jer. 14:11; see also 7:16; 11:14). There may very well be times when we should no longer pray for certain people since they have already been given up in this life to the judgment of God, and their lot is irreversible. It would appear that this is what John is saying in this verse. In practical terms, however, since we seldom can know if such is the case, we probably should not withhold our prayers in behalf of anyone. Who knows if the present blasphemer and persecutor of God may experience God's mercy in the same manner that Saul of Tarsus did?

7. The final question that we shall raise with regard to this verse, and the one which we shall discuss at length, involves the two kinds of sin mentioned. In particular we want to deal with the question of the "sin which is mortal." Apparently the sin which is not mortal is external, since it can be seen. Yet no attempt is made to describe or define either of these two sins. No doubt these terms were perfectly understandable to John's readers; but, unfortunately, the context in which John wrote and in which this letter was read is not known to us, so that we have great difficulty in trying to understand what John means by these expressions.

The expression "sin which is mortal" is literally "sin unto death." It calls to mind similar descriptions in the Scriptures. In Mark 8:38 Jesus warns that when he comes as the Son of man in all his glory, he will be ashamed of those who in this life are ashamed of him and his words. In Mark 3:29 we read of being "guilty of an eternal sin." This eternal or unpardonable sin is specifically referred to as blasphemy against the Holy Spirit, but, unfortunately, exactly what this eternal sin consists of is unclear. So it does not profit us to define the unclear meaning of "mortal sin" in our passage by the unclear meaning of "eternal sin'' in Mark 3:29. We find similar warnings in Hebrews 3:12–19; 6:4–6; 10:26–31; and 12:25–29.

In the history of the church numerous suggestions have been made as to what this sin unto death is. Some have suggested in light of Mark 3:29 that it refers to hardening one's heart so obstinately and so persistently against the influence of the Spirit of God that repentance becomes impossible. Others have suggested that it refers to a permanent rejection of the true faith in favor of paganism. Still others have suggested, in the light of the many exhortations in 1 John to love one another, that the hatred of one's brothers and sisters in Christ is meant. It has also been suggested that the Old Testament references to deliberate or presumptuous sins provide us with a clue. In the case of such sins there was no sacrifice permitted and death was often prescribed (see Deut. 17:12; Ps. 19:13; cf. Lev. 4:2, 13, 22; 5:15). In this regard we might also note that intentional sins resulted in excommunication from the Qumran community, whereas unintentional sins were punished with lesser disciplinary action (1QS 8:20–26).

It may be wise at this point to admit that certainty as to the exact meaning of ''mortal sin'' is impossible. A *possible* explanation may involve a group who had been members of the community to which John was writing, but who maintained a serious christological heresy and subsequently withdrew from the fellowship. These people were not of God, for they denied the incarnation of Jesus. They denied that Jesus Christ had come in the flesh (4:2–3). When their views were shown to be contrary to what the apostolic eyewitnesses were teaching (1:1–4), they withdrew from the fellowship. This proved that ''they were not of us; for if they had been of us, they would have continued with us'' (2:19). Here were people who had been brought into the most intimate contact with the people of God and the message of redemption. Yet they made an irreversible decision to reject the Light, preferring darkness instead. They had witnessed the working of God's power, yet in their hardness of heart they rejected the inward working of the Spirit, who sought to lead them to repentance and true faith. When God so reveals himself in power and conviction, there is no longer any excuse left. In referring to his past persecutions of the church, Paul points out that although he formerly blasphemed and persecuted and insulted God, he received mercy because he had acted ignorantly in unbelief (1 Tim. 1:13). Is Paul suggesting that if he had been aware that he was in reality opposing God, he would not have received mercy? Would such activity have been a sin unto death?

At this point we must emphasize that anyone who is in any way concerned about this issue need not fear that he or she is guilty of such a sin. Those guilty of this sin have no such concern and do not care about it at all. The very hardness of heart which leads to such a sin excludes any concern or regret in the matter. We can therefore be assured that if we fear we have committed the sin unto death, we have not committed it.

The Bible never discusses whether it is possible for a Christian to commit such a sin, or how sinful a Christian must be to be guilty of the sin unto death. Scripture is no more interested in discussing how bad a Christian can be and still be a Christian than it is in discussing how unfaithful a marriage partner can be before being guilty of adultery. Love for our marriage partner thinks only of how we can please him or her. Love for God likewise thinks only of how we can please him. The Christian keeps God's commandments (1 John 2:4–5) and does not abide in sin (3:6). The purpose of our text is to serve as an exhortation both to pray for believers whom we see sinning and to be aware that certain sins in this life may cut us off from the possibility of divine forgiveness. Needless to say, every believer like the psalmist of old should pray, "Keep back thy servant also from presumptuous sins; let them not have dominion over me!" (Ps. 19:13).

What Is Baptism for the Dead? (1 Cor. 15:29)

One of the most baffling statements found in Paul's letters is 1 Corinthians 15:29. In a context of defending the resurrection of Jesus in particular and the resurrection of the dead in general Paul asks, "Otherwise, what do people mean by being baptized on behalf of the dead? If the dead are not raised at all, why are people baptized on their behalf?" For centuries this passage has been a problem for the church, and any good commentary will list a host of suggested interpretations. The problem is due, of course, to the fact that nowhere else in Paul or the entire New Testament do we read of a baptism for the dead. At first glance the passage seems to refer to some sort of proxy baptism for dead people. In other words, it appears that Paul is referring here to a practice of experiencing baptism on behalf of people who have already died. Such a teaching would appear impossible to reconcile with Pauline teachings elsewhere which clearly associate baptism with a personal faith on the part of the individual for whose benefit the rite is performed (see Gal. 3:26–27).

One commentator has counted nearly two hundred different attempted explanations of this difficult passage. Among the more important attempts to explain the passage:

1. The interpretation of the early church explained the expression "on behalf of the dead" as a reference to the future resurrection of the dead; Paul was seen as saying that the people being baptized were baptized with a view to their own future resurrection from the dead. The problem with such an interpretation is that it assumes Paul intended that the words "for their own [future] resurrection" be inserted before the expression "on behalf of the dead." This would be a strange way for Paul to express the thought that those being baptized were being baptized with the aim of achieving their own future resurrection from the dead.

2. Some interpreters have suggested that the Corinthians were *wrongly* practicing a baptism for those who had already died and that, although Paul disagreed with the practice, he used it as an argument in support of his doctrine of the resurrection. In other words, Paul is saying something like, "How can some among you say there is no resurrection [v. 12] and at the same time practice [wrongly of course] a vicarious baptism for the dead?" A major problem with this interpretation is that there is no hint in our text that Paul is disapproving of this practice of the Corinthians, whatever that practice may in fact have been. It is furthermore atypical of Paul to build his arguments on a theological understanding or practice with which he disagrees.

3. Another suggestion is that our passage refers to the practice of vicarious or proxy baptism on behalf of dead Christians who for one reason or another had not been baptized. Some have even suggested on the basis of 1 Corinthians 1:14–17 that a number of the Corinthian Christians had not been baptized by Paul and had subsequently died. Again we encounter a serious problem with this interpretation: Baptism in the early church was so intimately associated with the conversion experience that unbaptized believers were a decided rarity. Conversion, as Acts clearly shows, always resulted in baptism. The claim that this baptism may have been for the stillborn infants of believers assumes among other things a clearly established practice of infant baptism by the 50s in the early church, an assumption which lacks any substantial New Testament support.

4. It has also been suggested that Paul's words should be interpreted as referring to the experience of people who became believers and were baptized because of the love and respect they had for Christians who had died. An example of this might be the promise made to a dying mother or father to become a Christian in order to be reunited in the resurrection day. It is also not at all uncom-

mon for the deaths of godly people to inspire others, even unbelievers, to take their place. The martyrdom of Nate Saint, Roger Youderian, Ed McCully, Pete Fleming, and Jim Elliot in January 1956 at the hands of Auca tribesmen is certainly a vivid example of this. Yet although permitting such an interpretation, our passage does not demand it and does not even suggest it.

5. Some scholars have suggested that Paul's words should be taken literally and that he is referring here to a vicarious baptism for the dead much like that of present-day Mormonism. Apparently such a rite was not unknown to the early church, but it was practiced only by heretics (so says Chrysostom). A major problem with such an interpretation is that it demands a sacramentalist view of baptism. Yet baptism is not regarded by Paul or the New Testament as an act which all by itself can bring salvation. Paul clearly refutes the view that baptism works *ex opere operato* (see 1 Cor. 1:14–17). In the New Testament, personal faith is always a requirement for salvation.

All sorts of other explanations could be listed, but it is clear that our text has withstood a satisfactory explanation over the centuries, and it is unlikely that the future will see any resolution of this difficult passage. In essence the problem lies not so much with what Paul said, but with the form of correspondence he used to say it. Adolf Deissmann demonstrated the essential difference between an epistle and a letter. It is quite common for people to use these terms interchangeably and refer randomly to the Pauline Epistles or the Pauline Letters. Yet there is a critical difference between these two forms of correspondence. In an *epistle* the writer assumes a minimum shared context between himself and his readers. He assumes, of course, their knowledge of the language (or access to someone who knows it), a general understanding of the meaning of the terms and the grammar he uses, and a general knowledge of the world about him which he shares with his readers. He does not assume, however, any special understanding between himself and his readers from which others are excluded.

On the other hand, in a *letter* the writer assumes a special relationship and understanding on the part of his readers to which others have no access. He builds on this knowledge and relationship, so that he does not have to explain certain situations, understandings, and knowledge that they have in common. An example of this occurred in my own life when my wife and I were overseas and received a letter from our daughter. In it she wrote something like, "We went out to eat, but we had fish because there was a fire again." Outside of our family this sentence makes little sense, for it builds on a common experience which our family shared but of which others are ignorant. We had gone out to eat at a Hardee's Restaurant, but there was a flash grease fire in the kitchen. So we went next door to eat at Arthur Treacher's Fish 'n' Chips. Our daughter was simply telling us that she and her brothers had gone through the same experience again. In a letter one builds on a common deposit of knowledge and experience; in an epistle one cannot assume such a deposit, and as a result great care is taken to explain each proposition and presupposition.

Needless to say, not all ancient correspondence can be neatly classified as perfect examples of letters or epistles. Romans is closer to an epistle, for here Paul is writing to a congregation he did not found and had never visited. So he does not build his argument on the assumption that his readers are intimately familiar with his theology. At times, however, he builds on a knowledge of the faith which he believes every Christian would have (see Rom. 6:3). On the other hand, 1 Corinthians is more of a letter than an epistle. It assumes all sorts of common information which Paul and the Corinthians share. It assumes even a previous letter (1 Cor. 5:9) as well as knowledge of Paul's person and ministry (1 Cor. 11:2; 15:1). As Paul wrote 1 Corinthians, he assumed a common core of information and background on the part of his readers on which he could build. Unfortunately, we are not privy to much of this information. In the case of 1 Corinthians 15:29 this is especially unfortunate, for Paul does not explain his reference to baptism for the dead. This problem is compounded by the fact that nowhere else does Paul (or the New Testament) use this expression or refer to such a practice. In fact his teachings on baptism elsewhere seem to conflict sharply with a literal interpretation of these words.

No doubt most Christians today would prefer that the Scriptures had been written as epistles rather than as letters. In the providence of God, however, the Spirit of God often worked through spokesmen living at specific times who wrote to specific congregations concerning specific issues. As a result, we must seek the specific meaning which the authors gave to their words within their particular context. Then we need to discover the implications of that meaning for us today. At times, however, we may lack sufficient information to determine what the author meant. In such instances we ought to be humble and admit that we know only in part. The Scriptures clearly reveal to us all that is necessary for our salvation and for godly living. They do not reveal, however, all that we would like to know. Nor is it possible to understand everything that the Scriptures teach.

First Corinthians 15:29 is one of those puzzling passages. We need to admit that we really do not understand what Paul meant by this verse nor how it fits in with his teachings elsewhere. In concluding our discussion it may be profitable to outline a general approach to take with regard to such passages:

1. We need to be humble and admit that we may not be able to understand the meaning of certain passages of Scripture. Rather than forcing on such a text a meaning which fits neatly into our system, we need to confess that we simply do not know of a satisfactory interpretation.
2. We should be careful not to build theological systems

on unclear passages of Scripture. Obviously it would be foolish to build a system of baptizing for the dead on this single and most confusing passage.

3. We should concentrate our attention and emphasis on the clear teachings of Scripture. The problem for most of us is not the passages of Scripture we cannot understand, but the Scripture which we understand quite well but do not take to heart and obey!

Scripture Index